Paul,
I appreciate
Leadership at S-
Andy

the ROAD to RELATIONSHIP

the ROAD to RELATIONSHIP

WRITTEN BY
ANDREW ALLEN

Tate Publishing & *Enterprises*

The Road to Relationship
Copyright © 2007 by Andrew Allen. All rights reserved.

This title is also available as a Tate Out Loud product. Visit www.tatepublishing.com for more information.

No part of this publication may be reproduced, stored in a retrieval system or transmitted in any way by any means, electronic, mechanical, photocopy, recording or otherwise without the prior permission of the author except as provided by USA copyright law.

All scripture quotations are taken from the Holy Bible, New International Version ®, Copyright © 1973, 1978, 1984 by International Bible Society. Used by permission of Zondervan Publishing House. All rights reserved.

The opinions expressed by the author are not necessarily those of Tate Publishing, LLC.

Published by Tate Publishing & Enterprises, LLC
127 E. Trade Center Terrace | Mustang, Oklahoma 73064 USA
1.888.361.9473 | www.tatepublishing.com

Tate Publishing is committed to excellence in the publishing industry. The company reflects the philosophy established by the founders, based on Psalms 68:11, *"The Lord gave the word and great was the company of those who published it."*

Book design copyright © 2007 by Tate Publishing, LLC. All rights reserved.
Cover design by Elizabeth A. Mason
Interior design by Janae J. Glass

Published in the United States of America

ISBN: 978-1-60462-137-2
1. Christian Living: Spiritual Growth   2. Christian Living: Practical Life
07.10.03

I would like to dedicate this book to my mom and dad and three grandparents. Outside of Christ they have been the greatest influences in my life, and they are still the only people I want to be proud of me.

TABLE OF CONTENTS

09	Introduction
13	My Relationship With God is a Struggle
27	Sinning Less is Not the Center of My Christianity
31	Service is Not the Center of My Christianity
37	Trials are Not the Center of My Christianity
55	The True Center of My Christianity
67	My New Perspective
71	Isolation
75	Meditation
83	Communication
89	Pouring Our Hearts Out To God
95	Sinning Less Revisited
99	Service Revisited
105	Trials Revisited
111	Self-Image Within Our Relationship
117	My Circumstances Do Not Define Our Relationship
121	The Deceitfulness of Our Emotions
129	My Need for Self Expression
135	Where Will I Seek God
143	Conclusion

INTRODUCTION

The religions of man have historically been based on seeking the blessings of gods. Every civilization that has ever existed has developed some religion, some means of attempting to influence the divine to use their power to benefit man, and in return man has offered his obedience, his adherence to the regulations of that god, the fruit of his labor, and even his very soul in the hope that he would be blessed on this earth and remembered when he leaves it. Man has developed many regulations, mythologies, and ceremonies to worship the gods that they believe exist. We have even gone to the extent of sacrificing our own species in an attempt to appease the gods, or receive their blessings.

The world's religions began when ancient man looked to the heavens and offered to bind themselves to something greater than themselves. They made covenants with what they hoped would be gods that brought rain on their lands to provide crops so that they and their families could survive, or to give them strength and protection against their enemies, or victory in battle. The covenants originated with man and were based on ritual and regulations. They were impersonal and tedious attempts to receive the blessings of distant and somewhat uninterested gods. The Lord set Himself apart from all other gods when He chose Abraham and made a covenant with him, a covenant that did not depend at all upon anything that Abraham did, but that was intended to be a testament to God's love and faithfulness. Unlike all other gods who are at the center of the world's religions, the Lord's primary desire is not sacrifice and ritual. He instituted these at times, but for very purposeful reasons designed to compensate for man's sin and to make man more knowledgeable of Him. Unlike any other god that was created by men, the Lord was able to initiate a covenant with man, and He did it because He loved us. He created us and desires us for one thing, a relationship with Him.

In the back of my mind I have always been aware of this, but quite often throughout my life as a Christian my focus and the center of my Christianity have been things other than that relationship. Thankfully the Lord is merciful, and He has led me down a narrow road that has been rocky, painful, exciting, desperate, and joyous to remind me that at the heart of all His planning, providing, and patient endurance is a desire to be intimate with me. This is a lesson I have learned over time, but is one that I will never let go of. In twenty-first century America, our Christianity has often been more affected by our culture than our culture has been by our Christianity. We have replaced relationship with many other things at the center of our faith.

In Revelation chapter two, Jesus commends the church in Ephesus for their great service and ability to discern right from wrong by using the word. However, in verse four, Christ identifies one fatal flaw in their Christianity by stating, "Yet I hold this against you: you have forsaken your first love." Contemporary Americanized Christianity quite often reflects the dynamic found in first-century Ephesus. We do so many things well and we are intimate with the word, and have a great sense of right and wrong, but God wants our undivided love more than anything else. James 5:4 states, "The spirit that he caused to live in us envies intensely." God desires complete commitment to Him. Our service, our knowledge, our activism, and our stand for what is right are all wonderful things, but they are not what God wants most from us. His greatest longing is for an intimate relationship with the only beings in the universe that were created in His image and likeness. We were created as beings who can be involved in fellowship with our creator in a way that is unique from all other aspects of creation. The most important thing that our generation, or any other can choose to do, is to learn to be intimate with God. If this is accomplished, then all other things in God's plan will end up falling into place. Without relationship at the heart of our faith, we face the danger of developing a hollow Christianity that is little better than the other religions the world has to offer. The following pages chronicle my struggle to restore relationship to the center of my Christianity; my intentions are merely to encourage whoever reads this, and perhaps to allow them to learn from my mistakes and the merciful things God has revealed to us all. I hope that you can relate to my experiences and that together we can become a generation that is daily pursuing intimate fellowship with our gracious and loving God.

MY RELATIONSHIP WITH GOD IS A STRUGGLE

I accepted Christ as my savior and asked Him into my life just a month prior to my eighth birthday. Faithful as always, He entered my heart in the form of His spirit and has resided there ever since. He has been such a daily and integral part of my life from that time forward, and I am so attached and dependant upon Him that I really can't imagine what life is like without Him. This fact is nothing to take pride in on my part, but instead is a persistent testimony to God's faithfulness. At times I feel that the only reason God continues to dwell in me is because He promised that He would. Genesis 6:3 and 5 describes God's attitude toward man prior to the flood. They say, "Then the Lord said, 'My Spirit will not contend with man forever, for he is mortal, his days will be a hundred and twenty years,'" and, "The Lord saw how great man's wickedness on earth had become, and that every inclination of the thoughts of his heart was only evil all the time." God, in His perfection, was unwilling to contend with the sin of mortal man, and He cleansed the earth by flooding it with water. These verses plainly show that our flesh is antagonistic toward God, and that our sin causes Him grief. Our sin and our flesh are something He must endure as long as our earth exists in its present state. Yet today, because of Christ, God is willing to contend with me and my sin on a daily basis as His Spirit resides within me. When I contemplate this I become very humbled and thankful that God is faithful and patient. The dynamic of a relationship between a perfect and holy deity and our corrupted nature, makes struggle an innate aspect of this relationship.

I know that God's thoughts and ways are not like mine, but I am amazed at how differently He acts and plans than I would if I were in His place. Sometimes I think that the greatest miracle God performs on a regular basis is that He allows His spirit to dwell in the hearts of man, and that He uses humans every day to accomplish His goals. To be perfect and holy, and to live in and use such imperfect and unreliable creatures, is a concept I continually have a hard time wrapping my mind around. If I were in God's place I would never endure such a poor home for my spirit, and I would never allow myself to be made so vulnerable as to trust such a flawed creature as man to be so actively involved in accomplishing my will. The struggle would be too annoying for me to bear, and I would most likely abandon the relationship. God acts in a completely different way, pursing us as far as He is able and graciously reaching out to us in love from His position of power, and as the offended party in the relationship. This act is completely contrary to how my human nature operates.

God's desire to live in me and use me has been such a mystery to me because I know the truth about myself, and

The Road to Relationship

what I am really like on the inside. At my very core I am naturally a creature of fierce passion, selfish ambition, and ungovernable independence and stubbornness. We are all born into this world thinking we are the center of the universe, and unless we are taught differently, we never lose this perspective. Even when we are taught differently, we continue to struggle with a nature that is bent on self-pursuit. Man is the most confounding paradox that has or ever will exist. We are the crowning jewel of God's creation made in His image and likeness, and yet we are rebellious and defiant toward Him. We were created for God's pleasure, but we all have sinned and all our sin is a hurtful and pain-filled move against Him. The earth and its resources were made as a home for us, and yet our sin has cursed it and brought evils into it that God never intended for us. What a mystery we and our nature are, even to ourselves.

How can we overcome this nature of ours? How can we function with any level of satisfaction in a world that was made not by us, but for us, but is corrupted by our actions and our selfish desires? How can we control our own passionate nature, or harness its energy and use it for something productive? I have come to the stark realization that I can do none of these on my own. My human and sinful nature dominates my will to do what is right. Outside of Christ, I am a creature owned by my self-centered wants and desires. The control and discipline that I desire over my heart, mind, and body can be experienced only in part, but as a whole is unattainable by me. Humans like to feel that they are in control of their own lives and destinies, but in fact, control of ourselves is one thing we can never possess. If we could control ourselves, then most of us would be quite different people than what we actually are.

There is a very simple spiritual law at work in us; we are controlled either by our selfish passions (our flesh or our sinful nature), or by God and the Spirit that lives within us. This law is simple, but it is played out in our lives in a most complex and often frustrating way. For myself, I know that God has my heart, and that He has had it for years, and that He will continue to have it until I leave this body and join Him. However, God is not a domineering task master who enjoys exercising totalitarian control over my life. Instead He is a very polite and genteel savior, and a very loving father. He has given me His Spirit, yet He does not force His will or desires upon me. Sometimes I wish He would; I wish He would remove my freedom to choose and just drag me down the narrow path that leads to salvation and productive living. I have a very acute knowledge of what is right and what is wrong, and I dearly love God's ways to my very core. I hate sin, and yet I am involved in it so regularly. I feel as though my right to choose is holding me back. I want God to make me quit sinning. I want Him to take away my ability to choose so that I can be free from the sin in my life that I hate so badly, but if my freedom to choose were gone, then the value of my relationship with God would be drastically diminished. As our creator however, He also knows well our nature and our human spirit, and He understands that such tactics would only lead to greater discontent and rebellion on our part. God is not interested in destroying our spirits; He is interested in conforming our nature to be like His.

One of the most humbling things that I have learned

about my relationship with God, is that more than anything else in the universe He desires my love and fellowship. What is really odd about this fact is that I don't have to give it to Him, and He has too much self-respect to just take it from me. I have found that when I give these to God, that what I receive in return is exponentially greater. This is one of the reasons I pursue a relationship with Him. However, I also find that my nature is not something that I master once and am done with. As good as the LORD is when I have tasted of Him, I still want to drink of my own fleshly desire. Here is the great conflict of our faith and our Christianity. What do I allow to control me? As I have stated before, I want to feel that I am in control of my own life, but that is never the case. Either God controls me and leads me into a life of great freedom and fulfillment, or I am controlled by my sinful nature, and enslaved and guided by its passions and desires. The fact that God's control over my life leads to freedom may sound like a contradiction, however, when I relinquish control to Him, the temptation and sin that I hate so dearly and fall prey to so often, begin to diminish. I become free from the innate control that my sinful human nature has held on me. In Christ, I am free from what destroys because I am controlled by what gives me life.

Ideally the choice to follow Christ is a one time decision that we make and that leads me through life always making the right decisions, and feeling comfortable and content in our relationship with Him. In reality, however, I have found that I am continually presented with the difficult decisions of daily life that I want to make for myself, with not necessarily any regard for what God wants for Himself and for me in those particular situations. I also find at times that I often have great regard for what God wants when I am making a decision, or am in a certain circumstance, but that it is often quite different from what I want. This is the struggle of faith that I find often characterizes my relationship with God. Cognitively it is quite easy to acknowledge that God's way is best, but our flesh burns fiercely in the seat of our human emotions and plays on our selfish feelings. It is relentless and possesses a never ending fuel supply from our desires. Thankfully, God is even more relentless and stubborn, unwilling to yield the hold He has on our hearts. The battleground for these opposing forces is my mind and the conflict is played out in my actions. I am often wounded or hurt in their struggle, but that is okay, for at that point God is able to remind me that He is a healer, and that my flesh and the one who tempts it seeks only to steal, kill, and destroy, as John 10:10 states.

For years I was frustrated by this struggle. I was often even discouraged at how difficult it could be to live a Christian life that is led by the Spirit. I was constantly confronted with what I felt was my perpetual failure to live up to God's standards and expectations. Christianity at times became a burden to me, but a burden that I was unwilling to let go of because I knew that it did provide a very fulfilling life at times, and because at my lowest points in life it had provided me with great comfort and peace. It also provided me with a purpose, and from it I gained wisdom that began to lead me to very successful and rewarding endeavors.

As I began to contemplate the struggle of being a Christian I found that I was not alone. Many of my faithful

Christian friends reported to me that they also feel that their Christianity is a struggle, often times on a daily basis. This was a comfort to me, but it also made me more determined to find a means to encourage them and myself through this. In consulting the scriptures I became encouraged, but also frustrated as well. I was able to see that the role models and heroes of my faith experienced the same struggle that I and my contemporaries face. In a very odd way, it made me feel quite relieved to read about the struggles that Abraham, Moses, David, Elijah, and all the other great characters of the Bible had in their relationships with God. If these men and women had doubts, fears, anxieties, and made mistakes, then the way I felt and faltered put me in pretty good company. I was encouraged by the realism and relevance of each of the lives I studied, and how much their relationships with God mirrored my own. My frustration persisted however, and at times even bordered on disillusionment. Though I never considered leaving my faith, I wondered if it would ever be what I and God hoped it would be.

As I continued to study individually and corporately with a small group of men who are very devoted to their relationships with God, I was reminded of God's awesome faithfulness. I also began to recognize the faults in my personal form of Christianity. I began to learn more what God desires and discovered that He looks at me in quite a different manner than I ever imagined. I learned that the struggle between my nature and God's will is never going to cease as long as I am in this body, but I also learned that it is something I can live with and something that does not have to be at the center of my Christianity. I was able to acknowledge and accept the fact that this struggle is actually characteristic of our faith, and if I ever cease to experience it on some level then my faith has ceased to move in the direction God wants. The struggle we feel is indicative of God's work in us. It is there because we are no longer instinctively following after our own fleshly lusts, but instead are actually attempting to resist them. To become a Christian is to start a war in your own mind and body. God living inside a creature of sin is not content with maintaining the status quo. He initiates change and our flesh resists with great fury. I hate the struggle, but if it ever ceases then so has my spiritual growth. I accept the struggle because it is a sign of my faith being stretched. I am also comforted by the fact that this struggle produces in me the characteristics that God needs me to have so He can use me to His full potential.

Those of us who follow Christ today are called Christians. This term was coined by nonbelievers in Antioch during the first century. It is a very complementary name that was given because of that church's attempt to closely adhere to the teachings and example of Christ. I find it much more interesting that when God chose a name for His people, the name He applied was, *struggle*. That is what the word *Israel* means, and He gave it to Jacob at Bethel because Jacob, "Struggled with God and man (Genesis 32:28)." A look at particular points in Jacob's struggle can be very valuable to us. You can track the growth of Jacob's faith by how he addresses and refers to God. In Genesis 27:20, when deceiving his father, Isaac, he refers to God as, "The LORD *your* God." His view of God is something that is attached to his father. He recognizes that God is able to grant success, and

The Road to Relationship

even credits Him with providing success on his errand, but from his perspective, Jacob views God as something that is his father's and not his own.

In Genesis 28 Jacob has his first personal encounter with God. He has a dream in which he sees angels moving between heaven and earth, and God speaks to him saying, "I am with you and will watch over you wherever you go, and I will bring you back to this land. I will not leave you until I have done what I have promised you." Jacob's response to this is quite interesting. He makes two very appropriate statements. In verse 16 he says, "Surely the LORD is in this place, and I was not aware of it," acknowledging that God exists and that his presence was quite obvious. In verse 17 he goes a step further by acknowledging that God's presence makes the place where he is holy by saying, "How awesome is this place! This is none other than the house of God; this is the gate of heaven." Jacob even follows his statements with rather appropriate action. In verse 18 it says, "Early the next morning Jacob took the stone he had placed under his head and set it up as a pillar and poured oil on top of it." Jacob made an attempt to commemorate his experience. This event shows that he now has a personal knowledge of God, and is even trying to take some appropriate action toward Him, but as we continue in the text we see that a real and personal relationship with God does not yet exist in Jacob's heart and mind.

In verse 20 we see Jacob doing what man has instinctively done with God throughout the ages; it states, "Then Jacob made a vow, saying, 'If God will watch over me on this journey that I am taking and will give me food to eat and clothes to wear so that I return safely to my father's house, then the LORD will be my God and this stone that I have set up as a pillar will be God's house, and of all that you give me I will give a tenth.'" Here Jacob attempts to negotiate terms, and bargains as though he possesses something that God desires. He expects God to prove Himself and if He does, then Jacob will be loyal and faithful to Him. This attitude sounds almost blasphemous, but essentially it is the stand that we continue to take today after we have first come to Christ, trusting Him to save us from our sin, but not completely trusting Him to be in charge of our decision making process. It is a perspective that we tend to battle often in our own struggles with God. Fortunately for us, God in His great mercy is willing to prove Himself to us. He is willing because we do possess something that He greatly desires, the ability to fellowship intimately with Him. His attitude from a position of power is so different than ours would be if we were in His place. Had Jacob responded to my promise with a negotiation, I probably would have permanently ended our relationship on the spot. God is so different however, and He understands the vulnerability and weakness of our human emotions. He continually reaches out and pursues us and proves His faithfulness to us over and over because He desires our intimacy so much.

As Jacob matures, his perspective of God is changed by God's faithfulness. In Genesis 31:5, he acknowledges that God is aiding him in his struggle with his father-in-law, Laban, by saying to his wives, "I see that your father's attitude toward me is not what it was before, but the God of my father has been with me." Again he makes the same confession when confronting Laban in verse 42 stating, "If the God of my father, the God of Abraham and the fear of Isaac, had not been with me, you would have surely sent me away empty handed. But God has seen my hardship and the toil of my hands, and last night he rebuked you." Jacob is conscious of God's work in his life and of the power and protection that He provides, but he continues to refer to Him as, "The God of my father," or, "The God of Abraham." He still has not truly personalized his faith. The relationship is lacking the deep intimacy that God desires.

In Chapter 32 of Genesis we see a great transformation in Jacob's view of God. Verse 7 describes Jacob as being, "In great fear and distress," and in verse 9 we see Jacob truly seeking God on God's terms for the first time in his life. He again finds himself in a struggle with man, this time it is Esau, his brother whom he had cheated and who he fears wants to take his life. Through verses 10 and 11 he humbly acknowledges God's hand on him and recognizes his unworthiness for what God has given, and in verse 12 he holds fast to the promise that God had made to him stating, "But you have said, 'I will surely make you prosper and make your descendants like the sand of the sea, which cannot be counted.'" In all his struggles Jacob is finally reduced to the point of trusting the only permanently consistent element in his life—the faithful presence of the God of his fathers. Here is where his true faith and his intimacy with God begin.

He encounters God that night and wrestles with Him physically in a way that parallels the struggle he has had spiritually. As daylight approaches, Jacob is unwilling to let go of God until he is blessed. In the same way we come to points in our life where we wrestle with God spiritually. We know God, we've seen His power, we've accepted Him as savior, we even can identify the work of His hand in our lives, but that is not enough for Him. He desires more. As in Jacobs's life, God uses circumstances to bring us to a point where there is no opportunity for negotiation, only acceptance of His complete control and sovereignty in our lives, and complete capitulation of our flesh. We wrestle desperately at these points because at the core of our humanness it is very difficult for us to actually let go of the fragile hold we have on our lives and trust that God will take care of us. Like Jacob, I personally have experienced those times when I feel very conflicted about my relationship with Christ, and my immediate future seems quite desperate. I struggle for control because I want things to happen in the way that I think is best, but in the end I simply hold on to Jesus as tight as I can because I know He is my only hope for salvation and success in what ever circumstances I find myself. To our human nature this position seems week, but the spiritual fact is that it is from this position that we, like Jacob, can receive a blessing and live under God's divine protection.

A great transformation takes place in Jacob after he wrestles with God. He is not just saved from the hand of his brother, but their relationship is restored. God proves Himself faithful once more and finally Jacob personalizes his faith. After he is reconciled to Esau, Genesis 33:20 states, "There he set up an altar and called it El Elohe Israel." This means, "God, the God of Israel." Jacob has become an intimate companion of God here. Like his father and grandfather before him, he has finally taken on the Lord as his personal deity and attached himself to God, beginning a period of close fellowship and faith that will last throughout the rest of his lifetime. Some struggles will still persist in his life, but never again will he view God as something distant, or identify Him as someone else's God. To him God is now *The God of Israel.* He exercises greater control in Jacob's life, which in turn leads to greater blessings, which in turn leads to deeper worship and the intimate fellowship that both Jacob and God desire.

Nearly four thousand years later I find myself in Jacob's place, struggling with a God whose great desire is to love me. Like Jacob, I am unwilling to give up the struggle regardless of the pain because I know at the end, and along the way, God is going to bless me. I'm sure God is often frustrated with me, even annoyed and disappointed, but He also has an underlying pride and joy in the fact that I won't let go of Him. I end up finding that the tighter I hold on to Him, the more I am aware of how great His grip is on me. The following pages are things I have learned so far about my struggle and my relationship with God. I have found that they are very characteristic of many humble Christians in twenty-first century America. My hope is that in some way they might be an encouragement to those who read them.

SINNING LESS IS NOT THE CENTER OF MY CHRISTIANITY

When I became a Christian, even though I was quite young, and at later points in my life when I desired to grow in my faith, I naturally felt that my first and most important duty was to sin less. After all, Christ came to earth in the form of a man, died a grueling death on the cross, and rose again on the third day so that I might have forgiveness of sins. If Christ's primary goal was to seek and save the lost, and He was the atoning sacrifice for my sin, then I determined that the most important thing I could do was stop sinning. In fact, at times I thought that the less I sinned, the more pleased and proud of me God would be. I thought that my personal purity may even make Him love me more. I even felt that my righteousness and my standing with God was somehow based on the amount of sins I did or did not commit. I couldn't imagine that there was anything He desired from me more than to see me sin less.

Because of this perspective, I set out to eradicate sin from my life. I had great plans to do this. I was brutally honest with myself and made a list of sins that I struggled with on a regular basis. I memorized scriptures that related to these sins, I prayed diligently for God to free me from them. I avoided temptations associated with them, and I even fasted in an attempt to conquer these sins in my life. As I did these things I began to see these sins become much less prominent in my life. I even got to the point of seeing some of them removed from my life for a time. I was so happy and elated that I felt I was actually beginning to live the abundant life that Christ talks about in the gospels. I also thought that God must be very pleased with me. I was excited about myself and my Christianity. My faith began to grow and I began feeling very good about myself and my relationship with Christ.

Then something began to happen. I realized that the rigid routine I developed to fight my sin was not maintainable. I got tired and at times complacent. Those sins I thought I had defeated for good began to resurface. I would go on an all out crusade to eliminate one, and then another would pop back into my life. I'd focus my energy on it, and the one I was previously working on became a problem again. My life became a constant juggling routine, and eventually I dropped all the balls.

A terrible thing happened at that point. I began to feel bad about myself. I felt like I failed God, and I began to view myself as a slave to these sins. From my perspective, my form of Christianity was failing, and I began to believe that God was disappointed and unhappy with me. I was a bad person and a poor Christian and I couldn't fix these facts. My self-esteem began to plummet and my faith was severely shaken. How could I be any kind of decent Christian if I couldn't defeat these sins?

Fortunately for me, I discovered some very important principles as I was studying God's word. As I read about the Old Testament law, I recognized that it was based on a written code and on the people's inability to obey it. The law has no ability to save, only to condemn. It was put into place to identify sin and to prescribe earthly punishments so that order might be maintained among the people. The commands and principles are holy and righteous, and they give life to those who live by them. However, the perfect God who instated them has a perfect standard that no one can live up to, therefore, all people sin and become breakers of the law. Their sins were set aside by the appropriate sacrifices, but never truly forgiven until Christ paid the final price on the cross. Because of this dynamic, their sin and imperfection was constantly before them, and undoubtedly became a burden for them to bear.

I saw how they continually failed and I began to see myself in their examples. The center of their relationship with God was a list of sins that they could not dispose of. It was always before them, and tangible and permanent redemption was only a shadow of what was to come. I saw that they were unable to keep the law and it was a burden to them that as a whole, they were unable to bear. The light bulb went off in my head at this point, the exact thing that Christ had come to free me from was what I recreated in my own life. I had reestablished a list of rules for my life that I was trying to live up to on my own, and this list of rules was completely contrary to my sinful nature. I had rebuilt in my own life the great burden that Christ had come to free me from. By focusing on sinning less, my list of specific sins had become the center of my Christianity. This is the furthest thing from God's real desire for my life. Christ came to remove my sins from me so I could fellowship freely with Him, and I took them back up and placed them between us, and our relationship was reflecting this dynamic. I was constantly focused on, and bringing up things that God had forgiven me for and forgotten ever occurred. I was essentially pouring energy, effort, and time into developing a solution for something that God already fixed. When I realized this I was humbled and embarrassed, and quite sorry I had been so focused on something that ultimately proved needless. I wondered how God felt about this. I'm sure He appreciated my effort, but I also imagine He could have received a much greater amount of enjoyment and satisfaction from me if my focus was in more appropriate areas.

As I began to discuss this process I discovered in my life, I found that many of the mature and devoted Christians I knew were doing, or had done, the exact same thing. They also had become somewhat discouraged and frustrated. In examining my own situation and discussing with others, it became clear that our mistake was in placing such great emphasis on sinning less. Don't get me wrong, sinning less is a good thing. It pleases God and it makes my life better, but sinning less was never meant to be at the center of my Christianity.

SERVICE IS NOT THE CENTER OF MY CHRISTIANITY

After my initial desire to please God by sinning less, I began to feel that the best way I could please God and be a good Christian was to do good deeds. If I did enough good things for God and others, then God would surely be proud of me, I would be happy and feel good about myself, and I would be living life to the full just as Christ had promised.

My desire and focus on good deeds was fostered by two things, the value of work ethic in my family and emphasis on work ethic in my church. In my family the importance of hard work was persistently taught and exampled to me by my parents and grandparents from childhood forward. I picked up the belief that if I worked hard enough, I could have whatever I wanted. My parents taught me that work was satisfying and enjoyable, and something I would do for the rest of my life. In their eyes being a hard and competent worker was one of the things they were training me to do. Work was preparation for adulthood and being a good worker was a skill that I would need throughout my life, in their opinion. These ideas also played a very influential role in my life. In fact, I began working for my grandfather on his hog farm at age nine, and worked six days a week through the summers until my dad started his own business and I began to work twelve hour days for him on the back of a trash truck.

My parents and grandparents also passed on the ethic of hard work to me by their negative and at times even judgmental attitudes about people who did not work hard, or failed to pull their own weight (this attitude in no way ever applied to those who were disabled in some way). It was offensive to my family to be a poor worker. My parents and grandparents always went the extra mile, and they always put out a great deal of effort in what ever they did, for themselves and for others.

When I got my first job outside of my family, my parents sat me down and told me that I had a responsibility to my boss to work my hardest at all times. They intensely stressed that if I were going to get paid for a job, I needed to do the job well and work my hardest at all times. I then got the same lecture from my maternal grandparents the next time I saw them, and the lecture was repeated by my paternal grandmother when she found out I had a job. There was no way a child could grow up in our home without recognizing that hard work was a very important value.

The church I grew up in and continue to attend also held the same value and expressed it in word and deed. I grew up in rural Southeast Kansas, and the little church I attend in a town of about two hundred and fifty people was congregated by conservative, blue collar men and women. Many were farmers or grew up on farms, and our leadership was mostly men who lived through the Great Depression. Hard work to them was as natural as breathing and you could never earn their respect unless you were willing to work.

They applied their work ethic to spiritual matters and church needs, and in my lifetime I was fortunate enough to see a little church in Tyro, Kansas, that barely ran a hundred in attendance each week grow into the largest congregation in our area with a current weekly attendance of well over one thousand. Our church worked at evangelism, it worked at Bible study, it worked at prayer, and it worked at meeting the needs of others. My grandparents' and parents' generations both thrived on the effort for some time. We went through numerous building projects and countless ministry programs. It almost seemed as though we willed the growth to happen. That of course was not the case, for as Psalm 127:1 states, "Unless the LORD builds the house its builders labor in vain." Our leaders and our congregation labored intensely, but not in vain. At our church, work ethic was next to Godliness in importance as a personal characteristic. At least that is the message I picked up as a child, adolescent, and young adult.

I naturally followed this pattern set for me. I enjoyed it and it came to me quite easily because of my home training. I poured myself into good deeds, ministries, and activities. I tried to be at the church every time the doors were open, and even at times when they weren't. I worked in and out of areas where I was gifted, and anytime some manual labor needed done, I usually showed up for the task. I reaped some wonderful rewards from this. People began to notice and respect me, I felt good about myself, and I was sure that I had to be pleasing God. In my mind, the more I did, the better Christian I was. I was following Jesus' advice by storing up for myself treasures in Heaven. I was a good Christian because I was a good worker. In my mind, being busy at good deeds was a sign of righteousness and there was nothing more important for me to do on this earth than work for God.

I did anything I could get my hands on. I did work that was both physical and spiritual. I often led three to four Bible studies per week, plus teaching on Sundays. I had an extensive prayer list of both micro and macro issues. I tried to encourage others, I tried to disciple younger adults; I tried to reach out to people in difficult situations. I thrived on manual labor and enjoyed being involved in whatever I could. I continued to grow spiritually, but my priorities were in the wrong place. All the things I did were good, but I had substituted them for intimacy with God.

This course of action worked for me for some time, years in fact. Then I began to discover that if work and good deeds are at the center of our Christianity, we become susceptible to some very human traps. At times I began to feel burned out. I was working hard on very spiritual things, but I was not necessarily refueling myself in the appropriate way spiritually. I often studied my Bible an hour or more a day and even prayed for that much time, but mere Bible study and prayer were not enough to sustain me. I felt good about helping others and being active, but I found that more and more my motivation was a sense of duty or obligation. As this feeling increased it began to reignite my human nature. There is a rebellious side of my humanity that does not like to have obligations, and is more concerned about pleasing itself than working for others. I eventually found myself still working hard, but with a very grudging attitude. I also found that a works-centered Christianity opens the door to pride. I began to feel very good about what I was doing, and the recognition I received from my deeds. I recognized my talents, as did others, and there was a great temptation to show them off, or take credit for them myself. Fortunately for me, God continually found ways to humble me and keep my perspective somewhat appropriate. I learned though, that pride is a fierce predator that is always near and crouching in preparation for an attack, and if we are not vigilant we can be devoured by it before we are even aware that it is present.

Another very important lesson I learned about having works at the center of my Christianity, is that eventually it will undermine my self-esteem. Each day that I worked on my Christianity I felt relatively good about myself, but if I had a day where I worked less, did something that was not overtly spiritual that was enjoyable, or just rested, I felt poorly about myself. I confessed and repented and begged God to forgive me for my lack of diligence and what seemed to me to be backsliding. My self-esteem and self-worth began to be dependent upon the amount of work I did for God. This became a vicious cycle that, had I continued, would have eventually made it nearly impossible for me to enjoy my relationship with Christ at all. It also might have destroyed positive thoughts or feelings I had about myself. This kind of thinking distances us from our loving father and paves the way for a works-based salvation and a very narrow perspective of God's wonderful grace. The lesson was hard, but I am very thankful that I learned that service is not at the center of my Christianity. The fact is, I don't want works at the center when I consider the ramifications of this dynamic. I don't want my relationship with God based on what I do because I am held back by my humanness and my physical and mental limitations. I also am much more interested in what God can give me, than in what I can work to achieve. Good deeds and service are important, but they should not reside at the center of my Christianity.

TRIALS ARE NOT THE CENTER OF MY CHRISTIANITY

A life in Christ is so radically different from my human nature and mind set, that often times it is difficult for me to understand it, let alone accept it. One of the most important ways that my faith differs from my nature is the way in which Christianity embraces trials. Christ was very up front about this. He told us in the gospels that if He was persecuted and suffered, we also would experience the same, as His disciples. James 1:2–5 and Romans 5:3–5 also tell us of the importance of trials and suffering and describe for us what they are designed to produce in our lives. On top of this all my biblical heroes and examples suffered in some form or another. It is quite clear that participation in the human race guarantees suffering, and Christianity often appears to embrace it and be quite fond of it. After all, Paul and Silas praised God after being beaten and thrown into a Phillipian dungeon. I was taught that our actions are to follow suit.

Let's face facts, there is no way to live and not experience some type of trial or suffering. Pain is as common to man as breathing. It affects us all regardless of culture or socioeconomic status. At some time in our lives we will all hurt, both physically and emotionally. We will all experience stress and most likely some type of trauma. No one is exempt and the consequences leave scars that can last a lifetime.

I am very fortunate that my parents taught me not to be consumed by the trials that I encounter in life. I learned from them that life kicks us all in the face and knocks us down, and part of what makes you a Christian is not staying down, but getting back up and persevering, regardless of how many times or how hard you get hit. I was taught that to quit was the only way that I could fail. I also learned that my suffering is part of what makes me like Christ. Christ's passion is the dearest part of the gospel message to me, and probably to most Christians as well. I also recognized that my suffering, if taken with the appropriate attitude, could be used to tear away at my nature and help me produce the characteristics of Christ in me.

I don't believe the intensity and the severity of trials can be judged wholly by us in this world. Trials come in many forms and the depth of the assault they make on our individual spirits cannot be determined in this life. Those of us living in the United States may not face the daily battle against starvation that some of our brothers living in third world countries face. We may not be threatened with persecution and death like the faithful in China, but we will be faced with suffering, and it may very well be as individually intense to us in our cultural setting as their trials are to them in theirs.

We humans usually respond to a trial in one of two ways. We either become overwhelmed by it and take it on as part of our identity, or we minimize it and are not in tune with the severity of its consequences on our lives. I am probably somewhat guilty of the latter. In the following paragraphs I am going to refer to the most significant trial of my life. I do this with some hesitation, and my goal is only to discuss the lesson of this chapter—the fact that my Christianity is not centered on my trials. I do not want to sound melodramatic, and I assure you that I do not feel my personal plight is any more or less difficult or intense than anyone else's. Again I want to stress that we all experience suffering, and only God is the judge of its severity and how well we handle it.

The origins of my most significant trial are still somewhat of a mystery and what I am relaying is the best guess of the doctors as to what happened to me. As a seventeen year old I was looking forward to my senior year in high school. For some reason that I can't put my finger on, I remember feeling a great boost in my self-confidence and self- esteem in the summer before my senior year. We were expecting to do very well in football and basketball, both of which I played, and I was fortunate to have a lot of friends and no real enemies at school. I attended a small consolidated school district where it was quite possible to literally know who everyone at school was. Our class was small, only about forty students graduated with me, and the average class size in those years at our school was between fifty and sixty. This meant there were only about two hundred kids in the whole high school.

When the year started off I was the picture of health and was starting to get into pretty decent shape for football. The week prior to our first game something completely out of the ordinary happened to me—I got sick. I had not missed a day of school since the sixth grade and I virtually never even had a headache or an upset stomach. However, one day at school I became inexplicably and quite acutely ill. I apparently checked myself out of school and drove to my grandparents' home, but didn't remember doing any of this. The next three days were a literal blur. I had a one hundred and five degree temperature and don't remember doing anything except sweating, aching, and periodically falling into a restless and uneasy sleep. I stayed at my grandparents' house most of that time. My grandmother was a registered nurse and she sweated over and observed me closely. All of a sudden after three and a half days, my fever broke, and being very inexperienced with illness, I assumed I was fine and immediately returned to my activities at school.

After a few weeks, with the illness barely a lingering memory from my recent past, my parents, family and I began to notice some odd changes in my activity level and my physical appearance. I began to notice that I was getting slower, and I was unable to make plays in football practice and games that I made earlier in the season. I also noticed that conditioning was getting more difficult instead of easier. My family noticed I was dragging, and when I started sleeping all day each Saturday and Sunday of every weekend, they began to suspect that something was very wrong. However, we all chalked it up to a busy senior year and thought I would eventually get rested and settle back into my usual active pace.

This didn't happen. Football ended and my fatigue increased. I also began to gain weight. I had never had an ounce of fat on me in my life, and all of a sudden my gut and my face both began to swell, and more mysteriously so did

The Road to Relationship

my legs, in particular my calves. My face would be so swollen in the mornings that my vision would actually be blurred for up to an hour after I got out of bed. I continued to not be myself physically and basketball practice, which I had always enjoyed, became a burden to me. Then my stomach and back began to ache on a nearly daily basis. I couldn't make them quit hurting. I drank an entire bottle of Pepto Bismol between classes one day, and it had absolutely no affect on my stomach pain. I then found that I could push my finger into my leg and it would sink. My grandmother reported to me that this was called edema. I was retaining water and had no idea as to why.

After a misdiagnosis from one doctor, who I was forced to go to by my basketball coach, I went to my family physician and he referred me to an urologist in Tulsa, Oklahoma. This doctor suggested a biopsy and told us it would be an overnight procedure. A few days before Christmas, I was taken by my mother to the hospital for the first time since my birth. I was awake during the biopsy and during one point felt an excruciatingly sharp pain. It lasted only a few moments and was gone. The doctor didn't seem overly concerned about it, so I didn't get too alarmed. Another one of our family values is tolerating physical pain and not allowing it to keep us from doing anything we deem important. The Allens were all raised to be tough during suffering. I hurt, but I could stand it. I found out later that night that I was just beginning to understand what *tough* really was. God was just starting to stretch me spiritually, and He was pulling on the part of my nature I was most in tune with, my physical body.

That night I was lying in a hospital bed with a sore back

from the biopsy, but expecting to go home the next day. It was a little painful to get out of bed, but I did and made it to the bathroom. Despite the urge, I was unable to urinate. I pushed and strained, but nothing happened. Then a paralyzing wave of fear crashed into my consciousness. There was something seriously wrong with me. There is something terrifying and humbling that occurs in the human psyche when a person realizes for the first time that their body is not performing the way it is supposed to. Despite my parental training to be tough and my youthful self-confidence, at that point in time I was nothing but a scared little boy, and fortunately I had a Heavenly Father whom I could turn to for comfort and support. In hindsight I realize that this was just the first small step in God teaching me that I am totally and completely dependent upon Him, a lesson that is unfortunately not finished in my life, and at times must be revisited. Sometimes even now, when I begin to pursue myself or become confident in my talents or abilities, God must return me to that state of mind. He does this not out of anger or judgment, but out of mercy, because when I am that scared little boy I will always seek the safety of my spiritual Daddy. When I am safe and comforted, I'll then begin to regain my bearings, I'll be reminded of God's great love for me, and I'll again look outside of myself and seek Him and His will with all my heart.

That night saw more difficulty. Not being able to use the bathroom meant that I had to be catheterized. Another new and humbling experience I would have to endure a total of seven times before the evening was over. Finally a surgeon had to insert the largest sized catheter they had. All this was due to the fact that there were blood clots in my bladder as a result of the biopsy, and they were preventing me from urinating. The large catheter allowed the clots to drain out of my bladder. My overnight stay lasted three days. I was sent home with no answers and feeling worse physically and mentally than ever. My follow up appointment with the doctor wasn't until three months later. I and my family were quite discouraged, and for the first time that I can ever remember, I was somewhat uneasy about the future. I realize now that God had to get me in this type of position before my faith in Him would ever be able to really grow and become practical and a daily focus of my life.

At home my condition worsened. I was extremely fatigued and unable to attend school, play basketball, or do anything that required any type of physical effort. My water retention became worse, and I gained so much weight that my appearance began to seem almost distorted. I looked like an oversized caricature of myself. I slept constantly and for the most part was unable to leave the house. I had no answers, no prognosis, and very little hope that things would improve. Finally with the help of some friends, my parents arranged for a meeting with another doctor in Kansas City, Missouri.

My appointment with Dr. Jim Mertz, who I still see regularly to this day, was no doubt divinely arranged. He admitted me to St. Luke's Hospital immediately after my appointment with him and began to treat the kidney disease that he felt I was suffering from. I went into the hospital weighing 177 pounds, and left ten days later weighing 132 pounds. Through IV diuretics they had removed forty-five pounds of fluid off of me in a little more than a week. I was diagnosed with Focal Sclerosing Glamarili Nephropathy. Essentially this meant that my kidneys were unable to appropriately filter the protein in my blood. It apparently had started as a residual effect of the virus I had a few months earlier that caused my high fever. I had seemingly never quite recovered from it, and it settled in my kidneys and started a very destructive process.

I was encouraged after leaving the hospital, mainly because I was at least looking normal again. However, at 132 pounds, I had actually lost sixteen pounds of muscle since my football physical in August when I weighed 148 pounds. I felt better, but was still quite weak and often fatigued. I was put on oral steroids and diuretics to help fight the symptoms of the disease. I returned to school and attempted to return to basketball. I made a valiant effort at both, but my condition would not allow me to continue the physical effort required from sports, and I ended up missing more days of school the second semester of my senior year than I was able to attend. The edema returned and I was forced to alter my diet. I could only take in two grams of sodium and one quart of liquids per day. These restrictions made my diet nearly impossible. I could eat nothing out of a can or box, no fast food, and very little bread, butter, or condiments. This was a drastic change in my life style, losing my ability to both be active and my ability to eat what I wanted. Along with these two factors I also started experiencing severe muscle cramps. I would get them in all parts of my body from my jaw down to my toes. Any physical activity I attempted during the day would have painful consequences in the form of these cramps later in the night. This added greatly to my frustration and discouragement. The worst was yet to come.

Later that spring I returned to the hospital to receive IV steroids in an attempt to slow the progression of the disease, or possibly cure it. My physical symptoms did improve some, but at an awful price. My appearance was altered terribly as a side effect of the steroids. My face swelled, my muscles seemed to grow even thinner. I developed a layer of fat around my midsection and I began to look completely different than I had only a few months earlier. I could barely stand to look in the mirror, and I still have trouble today looking at my graduation pictures, which were taken at the time my *moon face* and overall appearance was most affected by my treatments. All the confidence and positive self-esteem I'd begun to develop the previous summer was now gone. The steroids were also affecting my moods, making me somewhat irritable and on edge. These symptoms were compounded by my fatigue, and my attitude in general began to take on a negative tone.

By now all my denial was broken down, my hope for salvaging my senior year was gone, and my outlook was grim. Thanks to my parents and my faith, I continued to attempt to live as normal a life as possible. Then I suddenly began to feel a little better. I was able to start junior college and I could even do some activities on days I felt up to it. Although I often continued to pay the price my sick body demanded when I was active. The cramps never left, and if I had the energy to do something one day, I usually had to spend the next day recovering.

During the next two years I was able to complete junior college. My concentration and energy levels were frequently poor, but I did relatively well. My looks eventually returned to normal as the large doses of steroids ceased to be an effective treatment. The cramps and low energy never left and progressively got worse. I began to require regular hormone shots because I was becoming anemic. I enrolled and started classes at a four-year college, but halfway through the first semester my condition worsened to the point that I had to be put on a dialysis machine. This form of dialysis did not agree with me, and my health was maintained, but my ability to function was quite impaired. I had to quit school. My energy level was terribly poor and there was just no way I could attend a full day of classes and keep up on homework and studying.

I decided I wanted to try peritoneal dialysis to see if I could tolerate it better. I underwent a short surgery to insert the necessary tube into my peritoneal cavity, which also partly hung outside of my body. A solution entered my body through the tube, and I was required to change this solution three times per day. By this means I was able to filter out some of the waste products and impurities in my blood that my kidneys were no longer able to remove.

The process of changing the solution took some time. The solution inside my body had to be drained out, and another had to be poured in through the tube. There was a very high risk of infection, and I had to be very careful when changing out my solutions. My activities were limited by my lack of energy, and also by the fact that I had a tube protruding from my stomach area. I felt a little better, but the disease had progressed. School was definitely not an option, and we were beginning to plan for a transplant.

Somewhere during this time, at the age of nineteen or twenty, I came to the realization that my life was never going to work out the way I had planned, or hoped it might. I also accepted the fact that many of the dreams I had for my life were not ever going to come true. I feared that my life would be one constant battle with poor health. I couldn't remember what it was like to feel good physically, and when you endure constant pain and fatigue, you also begin to acquire emotional symptoms as well. I was discouraged and frustrated. Even with an upcoming transplant there were no guarantees, and I really wasn't expecting a profound improvement in how I felt, only the prolonging of my life as it currently existed. I was living day to day because I couldn't bear to look into the future.

This entire period of my life became very significant. When faced with these ongoing trials I began to turn more and more to God for help. As I said before, I grew up in a Christian home with good Christian parents. I attended a booming little church that grew into a rather large church in relationship to its community. I was active in the church and had the benefit of many good teachers and examples. I accepted Christ at a relatively young age, and for most of my life I had the benefit of the Holy Spirit dwelling inside me. For the first time in my life I had to make a real decision about the prominence of my faith in my life. I could no longer ride the coattails of my parents or the people at my church. I had to take ownership of my individual faith and begin to live and act upon it for myself. This was somewhat frightening, but it became quite exciting. I was to the point where I really began to understand that Christ is important not just as a savior or the answerer of prayers, but also as a comforter, a guide, and a friend. I was making my faith something that was my own, truly unique and personal to my life and my particular situation. God had become real to me.

I decided to take Christ more seriously. I began to pursue Him, often out of desperation and because I felt I had no other choice, but as I pursued Him, He allowed me to taste the goodness that a real individual relationship with Him brings. Once I began to taste and experience this, I would never again be able to leave it alone.

In our daily struggle with our human and sinful nature, there is no greater means that God has to break down our flesh than trials of some nature. They produce in us characteristics necessary for effective Christian living such as perseverance, endurance, faithfulness, and most importantly dependence. I am at all times dependent on God for all my basic needs, I often just don't acknowledge it, or fail to recognize it until I am involved in some type of circumstance that is greater than me. Trials acutely affect my perspective of me and my true relationship to God. I remember that I am merely dust that He has breathed into, fragile, full of flaws and easily damaged, and that I have no real control over anything that happens in the universe. I am reminded that He cares for me, that He is merciful, and that He will never leave or forsake me. In fact, He uses difficult circumstances to draw me closer to Him and show me He was not just a savior on a cross two thousand years ago, but that He *is* a savior who can deliver me from any current emotional or mental anguish.

God's readiness to save has always been one of the characteristics that endeared Him to His people. God's faithfulness and mercy are most evident in the lives of our spiritual predecessors when they were in their time of greatest need. We see a change or growth in their relationship with God at points when they were in situations that required divine rescues. We've already discussed this with Jacob, but David grew close to God when he was fleeing the hand of Saul, Paul while he was in a Phillipian dungeon, Daniel when he spent the night with lions, Joseph while toiling in slavery, and Moses when he was trapped against the Red Sea. All these are examples of God using circumstances to prove to his people that He is their faithful and gracious redeemer. He cannot prove these things however, unless He allows us to experience situations that give us cause for human fear.

Some very strange things also begin to happen to me in the midst of trials. The fruit of the Spirit begins to flourish in me, mainly due to the fact that layers of my fleshly nature are ripped away. In the presence of turmoil I am able to feel great peace. This makes no sense in human terms, but as I begin to let go of what control I feel I have, the Spirit begins to compensate and reveals to me the characteristics of Christ and helps me experience and live them out in my daily life. When I am in turmoil, the Spirit provides peace. When I am in stressful and painful circumstances, the Spirit allows me to be joyful. When I am at the end of my rope, the Spirit exercises patience. The greatest yields of the fruit of the Spirit come when the ground of my human heart is torn by the plow of trials. The fruit of the Spirit is of course listed in Galatians 5:22 and they are love, joy, peace, patience, kindness, goodness, gentleness, and self-control. These are not natural to my human nature, but when trials begin to strip that nature away, the Spirit is able to work in its place and this fruit becomes more evident in my life. Ultimately, it begins to dominate the areas where hate, envy, rage, bitterness, and malice once ruled.

Trials are the great catalyst for real spiritual growth in the lives of Christians. Trials serve to break down my flesh and intensify my focus on God. In turn, where my flesh once ruled, the Spirit now is free to work and produce its fruit in my life. As I experience this fruit I enjoy it and am comforted by it, and I begin to love, appreciate, and seek God more. My relationship expands and becomes more and more fulfilling. God means more to me because I realize He is most faithful when my need is the greatest and I have to be in some degree of distress before I can appreciate His faithfulness and comfort fully.

There is another very subtle, and yet fascinating and important thing that God does in trials. He reframes our perspective of them. In my work as a mental health professional, I have dealt with people who were encountering various types of trials, from abuse to divorce, to the death of loved ones. I have found that people deal with trials best when they can find a reason for them or some kind of purpose within them. God provides both of these for those of us who are Christians. The general reason for all trials is that we live on a cursed earth. Life is not fair, fortunately for us, or we would all taste eternal death as a result of our own personal sin. When we accept the fact that our sin brought hardship into our lives in a general sense, then we understand there is a reason why bad things happen—even to *good* people. Beyond this however, is a purpose our trials bring with them. As I have alluded to already, it produces in us characteristics that we need. James 1:2–5 and Hebrews 12:4–11 describe how Godly traits are produced in us through trials. Another very important purpose that comes with trials is that they make us like Christ.

Christ suffered without cause and was tortured and killed at the hands of men He created. He was ridiculed, slandered, made fun of, and in the time of His greatest need he was abandoned by His closest friends. I could go on endlessly about the sufferings Christ endured, not just physically, but like us also mentally, emotionally, and spiritually. His suffering brought Him to the point of tears on more than one occasion, and He also suffered in a way that is beyond our understanding due to the fact that He was our perfect and Holy God living in fleshly form. Experiencing temptation that He had never known before created a type of suffering that we who have constantly been tempted cannot relate to or imagine. Our Lord suffered also at the inappropriate responses to Him, and the rejection of Him by His own people. Christ's life was full of suffering. As I suffered through my trials and recognized the purpose in them, my Christianity began to take off. In fact, my trials were the greatest catalyst I ever experienced in the growth of my faith. I began to see not just how God used them to affect me, but also that He was using them to impact the lives of others. Even though my situation was very stressful and frustrating to me, I knew it was not in vain, and I was able to endure it because there was purpose behind it, just as there was behind my Savior's suffering.

Fortunately for me, dialysis was not the ending treatment of my kidney disease. My father willingly donated me one of his kidneys and, in February of 1991, I underwent a kidney transplant. I did not know how this would affect me, and my expectations were quite low. I was going to be happy just to return to some level of physical freedom and activity, and hopefully be off of dialysis. The operation was a success and

I began my recovery in the hospital without incident for the first few days after the surgery. As soon as my parents finally left the hospital I began to have complications. My lungs began to fill with fluid for no apparent reason. I was taken to ICU and during the next two days I was examined by more than twenty doctors, started on five antibiotics, and eventually placed on a ventilator and nose tube. The doctors were at a loss as to what was happening, and my physical condition continued to deteriorate to the point that my parents were told by the doctors that *if* I were alive the next morning, I would be in a coma.

My parents received this news on a Wednesday and began calling my relatives so they could see me one final time if they wished. I was in and out of consciousness that day and evening, and each time I woke up I saw a new set of aunts and uncles, cousins, grandparents, and friends. I quickly concluded why I was receiving such attention, but I was in such pain when I was conscious, that the thought of death and joining Christ presented no fear, and would have been a welcome change. Word of my condition reached our church in Tyro and at the service that Wednesday night they held a special prayer service just for me. My parents left the hospital that night distraught, expecting to come back the next morning and find me in a coma or dead. God had a different plan, however, and through prayer and God's great mercy and grace, I was alive, awake, and feeling quite well. Each doctor who examined me the day before returned and had no explanation for my immediate and complete recovery. The antibiotics were stopped, the ventilator and nose tube removed, and I was conscious with no pain and no problems.

The Road to Relationship

Later I learned of the prayer meeting and of many others who prayed outside of that meeting for my healing. Many of those people commented to me on how God strengthened their faith through my healing. This was a great and humbling lesson for me. God could and was using my circumstances to create situations in which He could bless others, and I didn't even realize it. It again shook my perspective of God and my perspective of myself. It brought new light to Romans 8:28 and it made me conscious of the fact that the *good* God is working toward may not be devoid of pain. This impacted my faith and my Christianity. During the previous few years I placed my trials at the center of my Christian life. I associated my suffering with God's work in my life, and in the lives of others. I was humbled and quite satisfied by the fact that the difficult things I had endured were used by God for His ends. I also had drawn much closer to Christ—I had a fellowship of pain with Him. As He suffered for the glory and purpose of God, so had I, although it was on a much lesser level. This opened the door for me in many new areas of my Christian walk. I sought God more; I studied His word more; I prayed more, and I wanted to serve Him more. The impact of these events became obvious to everyone around me. I felt devoted and in love with God to a degree I could never have experienced outside of these trials.

I had some physical issues that lingered for a few years, but were eventually ended with a change in medications. Although, I never got back to the level of physical functioning I had prior to the transplant, for the next decade I enjoyed good health and a productive life. I was able to finish college, begin a career, and later went back to school and completed a master's degree. I was rarely sick, functioned quite normally, and most people who met me had no idea I had a transplant unless I told them, and usually I didn't. I was able to view it as something that I had endured, not something that dominated my life. As the trial began to dissipate, I found that there was a void in my Christianity. My growth slowed and my passion for Christ became less intense. The daily struggles that had forced me to keep sharp and on guard were gone, and a level of complacency crept back into my life. The constant sense of purpose I felt in my suffering was also gone, and I had to find something to replace it with. I tried many things, but incredibly nothing gave me the same sense of closeness to God and as clear a reason for living and being a Christian as my trials had done. I don't like trials, but they are a necessity for real spiritual growth. In them I am drawn closer to Christ and closer to the reality of my dependence upon Him. They are essential for stripping away the layers of my flesh, but they are not the center of my faith or my Christianity, no matter how meaningful and dear God becomes to me when I am in the midst of them.

THE TRUE CENTER OF MY CHRISTIANITY

As I have discussed, for years I acted on what I was taught, or what I thought God wanted from my Christianity. I found that sinning less, service, and trials were very important aspects of my faith, but they were not the center of my Christianity. I began to realize that despite my good intentions and my pursuit of God, often times with great zeal and passion, I developed the wrong perspective of my faith. I had a very good grasp on Christian doctrine, and I was very secure in what I believed and why I believed it. Jesus was the Lord of my life and I received many great blessings from my faith and God's grace. However, when I began to really examine my faith and my motives deeply, being brutally honest with myself and God, I found that my general perspective was that I was a follower of Christ because of what He had done and could do for me. I was still quite focused on what I could get out of being a Christian. This is not entirely wrong, and this perspective is one that I have found most Christians possess. It does not mean that I am lost and does not discount the work Christ has done in and through my life. It is not, however, the optimum perspective that we can have as Christians.

Is God getting the optimum from my life? This has been one question that has haunted me throughout adulthood as a Christian. It is also a question that has motivated me significantly in all the areas that I have discussed previously. My greatest fear in Christianity has always been that I will not accomplish the tasks that God has prepared for me to do in this life. I have lived in fear of being a failure in the eyes of God. The guilt that Christ died to remove from my life has persistently dogged me, and I have constantly asked myself, *Have I done enough?* That works-centered Christianity that destroys my self-esteem and distances me from God is hard to let go, and as long as I looked at Christianity from this perspective I would never be free from it.

I then began to ask myself some very important questions about the author and perfector of my faith. If Christ's main goal for me is not to sin less, serve more, or endure trials, then what does He want from my Christianity and my life? This was the right question, but I was unable to answer it correctly. I continued to ask it every time I studied, when I prayed, when I worshipped God. I fervently attempted to look at Christianity from His side. This opened a whole new door of understanding for me. My question was not answered immediately, but over time it became clear what God wanted. It was surprisingly wonderful, but also somewhat difficult for me to accept.

Two verses that I had been aware of for years became the catalysts for changing my perspective. I Peter 1:20 and

Revelation 13:8 state that Christ was the chosen sacrifice before the world was even created. As I began to contemplate this fact, my theology and my understanding of God both changed dramatically. I always believed that God created a perfect earth to be inhabited by perfect people. Adam sinned and we in turn followed suit, and Christ was then set apart as a sacrifice to restore our relationship with God. This, however, is not what I Peter 1 and Revelation 13 state. They say that Christ was set apart and chosen before man was ever created. Christ was not a compensatory *Plan B* that came into effect as a result of man's sin, He was *Plan A*. This thought, and its ramifications, absolutely floored me. God in His infinite knowledge knew that man would sin and that He would have to sacrifice His son to restore His relationship with man, and He created us anyway. *Why?*

I asked myself this question over and over and the fact is: in this body I will never understand fully the answer to that question. I am able to know this, however—God desires a relationship with a being of free will that He created in His own image and likeness so much, that He would endure sin, a curse upon His creation, thirty-three years on earth in a fleshly body, and the death of His only son to have and maintain that relationship. I finally discovered what should be at the center of my Christianity—my relationship with God, which comes through Christ. Any and everything else is preceded by this. Our relationship is what Christ wants at the center of our Christianity, it is what our entire faith and religion is built on and is all about.

When I realized this it led to one of the most wonderful and amazing feelings I have ever experienced, but I had an extremely difficult time accepting this fact and living accordingly. When I realized that my purpose in life is to have a relationship with the all- powerful Creator of the universe, I was extremely humbled and rather terrified. I was humbled because I know how bad I really am. I am acutely aware of the passionate nature of my flesh, of my innate rebellion against God and His perfect ways, and of my utter failure to live up to his Holy standard. I knew that He desired and had a relationship with me, but I was terribly unworthy of the close and intimate relationship that he desires to have with me.

My unworthiness was not a new concept to me. I knew I was saved by grace through no work of my own. I knew I deserved eternal punishment for my sin. I knew that God sent Christ out of His amazing and wonderful mercy, but this is where my knowledge ceased. I was always thankful for Christ and for the fact that His sacrifice had saved me from Hell. My view of God ended here. It was nice; it was enough to build my faith on. I felt very indebted to God for good reason, and also very appreciative of Him, but despite my attempts to please Him I never got beyond the point of what He had done for me. I never thought through the idea that he received something that is very wonderful and special to Him, not just from my service, but also from our personal relationship. I never thought I could be an intimate friend of the divine.

I still have trouble with this thought and it is difficult for me to even express it. The fact is, this is the desire of God's heart. He wants to be our intimate friend. He did not sacrifice His only son to obtain more servants, these He had in myriads. He sent Christ to save His children so we might grow up into spiritually mature adults who can be His companions and fellowship with Him now and for all eternity. Our fellowship is craved by God. He loves us above all things except Christ. He receives a blessing from our freely given communion with Him that exceeds any joy He has from all other aspects of His creation combined. He loves us and He is fulfilled when we return the love in our relationship with Him, through intimate fellowship.

As I said before, this is an awesome and wonderful thing, but I am also terrified by it. I don't know how to be a friend to God; I am quite often a poor friend to those on earth that I care about. My first inclination is that I must work at being God's friend, but I know that this is wrong because I do not have to work at maintaining my most treasured human friendships. These friendships are often informal and casual. I never greet my best friends with a handshake. If we don't talk for days, we can easily pick up where we left off the last time we were together. Our relationship with God is somewhat like this, not that we should be nonchalant with Him or go days without communication, but we can be completely personal, relaxed, and able to enjoy ourselves in His presence. I have to fight my human desire to bring ritual and ceremony into the relationship, and I must remember that a relationship built on love is something that can happen very naturally and aspects of it are quite spontaneous and unplanned. My intellect, and my selfishness, and all my human characteristics have the potential to get in the way of me having interaction with God that pleases Him. God knows how to run the relationship in the best way for the both of us; I just have to be an attentive and willing friend.

The difficult thing about having this type of relationship

with God is that He is still God, and I am still human with all my faults and weaknesses still in tact. Our relationship with God is complex, but He meets us where we are at and He manifests Himself to us in the exact way we need Him. It is not always the way we want Him, but it is always the way in which He knows we need Him the most at the time. At times I need God as a savior, at times as a father, at times as a master, and at times as a friend and confidant. There are many more ways in which I have a need for God, and He is always faithful and close at hand. I am acutely aware of what I want from God at all times, and quite often aware of what I need from Him. However, I am afraid that I am frequently very poor at knowing what He really wants and needs from me. My focus in our relationship tends to be very one sided. I think this is because, after all these years as a Christian, I still have a hard time grasping how much I mean to God, and understanding and accepting that I bring Him great joy and satisfaction.

When I think about my relationship with God, I am immediately confronted with His great holiness. This in turn makes me aware of my sin and my humanness. From this perspective I feel a significant distance between God and myself. I can't be God's friend from this distance. This is my perspective, but it is not necessarily God's. I have to remember that the purpose of sending Christ was so my sin would not always be before God, making it possible for me to draw near to Him. He sees no sin in me because of the blood of Christ, and the intimate friendship and closeness that I desire is attainable. It is also something that He desires, maybe even more than I do. Christ has made it possible not just to approach God at anytime without ceremony or ritual,

The Road to Relationship

but also for Him to reside in me in the form of His spirit. I am never out of God's presence because He lives in me, and nothing can separate me from God and His love. If there is distance in our relationship, even if it is merely distance that I perceive, then it is not the relationship God desires from me. If God didn't want an intimate friendship with me, He would have never allowed His spirit to dwell in me. If the thought of my sin dominates my view of our relationship, then I have not taken hold of the depth of Christ's sacrifice, and God is being cheated out of aspects of my fellowship that He desires to experience and enjoy.

I think it is very important to consider God's motivation for creating man, when we contemplate our relationship with Him. We must remember that God has no peers. He did not grow up with anyone, He did not play little league or high school ball with anyone, He did not go away to college and join a fraternity. To have friends or fellowship, God must create someone or something to be friends and fellowship with. This apparently is not the angels, for the writer of Hebrews tells us that they are, "Ministering spirits sent to serve those who will inherit salvation" (Hebrews 1:14). They are sent to serve us. Peter also tells us that we will judge angels. With these facts in mind, and considering that God designed and created us in His image and likeness, it becomes obvious that we are His choice as the primary source of His friendship and fellowship. What an unbelievable source of encouragement and delight. I can't imagine being created for anything more wonderful.

How then do I respond this fact? As I have already stated, I continue to be confronted with my sin when I think about my relationship with God. After considering such things, my outlook on Christ's sacrifice and grace has begun to change. I can see now that what God desires is that I allow that sacrifice to truly free me of guilt and even consciousness of my past sins in our relationship. If my sins are interfering in my perspective of our relationship, it is because I have dragged them along with me—God has already forgotten them. I have to approach God with the knowledge that I am perfect in His eyes, and that He created me for fellowship with Him and has done everything in His power to make it possible to be His friend. Sure I am unworthy of this, but remember, God has no peers, and anything He creates will be unworthy of this, but it is what He wants.

Okay, now that I can begin to accept the fact that God wants me to be His friend, another imposing question enters my mind. *How do you be a friend to a deity?* My initial response is, "By obeying Him," but this again puts service at the center of our relationship. Obedience is important and it is part of having the relationship with God that He desires, but it is not the center of the relationship either. Have faith is my next thought for, "Without faith it is impossible to please God" (Hebrews 11:6). Faith is vital, but it is an often misunderstood and ambiguous concept, and often I lack the amount I need. I needed something simple and practical to move deeper into this relationship with God that we both desired. As I continued thinking about the first step in a relationship with God, I thought about what was necessary to build and maintain a relationship with one of my human friends. It appears to me that the first and most vital step to establishing a relationship is spending time with each other. In fact, I think this is exactly what God desires from us.

The Road to Relationship

There are some things that I have noticed about my relationship with my earthly father that have taught me very important lessons about the dynamics of my relationship with my heavenly Father. I can only remember one, or maybe two times in my entire life that my father sat down and had a talk with me about some specific issue. Yet, somehow I picked up his morals, his ethics, and his values, even some of his mannerisms. I catch myself today saying things that sound just like comments I have heard him make throughout the last thirty years. I also picked up some of his bad habits and negative perspectives. How is this possible when he took such a little amount of time to sit me down and instruct me?

The answer to this question is *baseball*. Well, it is not really *baseball*, but that's what I primarily associate the answer with. From the time I was about eight years old, through the time I was about twelve years old, my dad worked at a bank and was usually home by 5:00 p.m. Everyday from March through October of those years, if the weather permitted, he played baseball with my brother and me, and often times our cousin, in our front yard. We had base paths worn into the yard that grass didn't grow in for years after we stopped playing. We played from the time he got home until dark. Our games were as routine a part of our lives as eating and sleeping. On top of this, he would take us with him to the softball tournaments he played in on the weekends. He was home for dinner every night, even as we got older. He came to all our activities through high school, and when we stopped playing baseball, he picked up other hobbies we enjoyed, such as fishing. He also involved us in activities that he enjoyed and when he started his own business, we were a part-time labor force. I relay all this to illustrate a very important spiritual principle that was played out in my relationship with my physical father. Time together builds relationships and this is our starting point for having the kind of relationship with God that He desires. I can't remember many important talks my dad had with me because they weren't all that necessary. I picked up his morals, values, and habits because I spent so much time with him. He didn't have to plan *quality time* with me because it naturally occurred out of the quantity of time he spent with me. He achieved many of his goals in parenting, and I learned the lessons he was trying to teach because the opportunity to learn was so frequently present.

I think my relationship with God plays out in a very similar way. Our relationship grows and is fueled by me spending time with Him. The great thing about this relationship is that I don't have to wait until God gets home from work, or for the weekend to arrive. He is accessible at any time and any place. He even dwells inside me. God makes Himself so accessible to us for a reason—He desires our intimate fellowship. It is an awesome thing to have the God of the universe so close and so interested in all that we do. If all God wanted was to save us from hell, have us as His workers, and eventually restore the earth to perfection, then He would have had no need to give us His spirit. He gave us the Spirit so we could experience and fellowship with Him more deeply and freely. Jesus describes the Spirit as a comforter in John fourteen, again noting that God uses Him to meet our most basic emotional needs.

The truest and deepest friendships require the participants to allow one another into the most personal aspects of their lives. To be a friend requires a great trust, which in turn means you make yourselves vulnerable to each other. You risk the secrets of your heart and the dreams of your mind allowing someone else to have knowledge of them. The most guarded treasures of your soul are brought out for review. You open yourself up to the possibility of great pain from possible criticisms, dismissals, critiques, or even abandonment by someone else. God has done all of these things with us. He has put His great love for us and His desire to fellowship with us on display. We reject Him and pursue our flesh, turning our noses up to His desire for a relationship with us. Even when we do this He does not stop seeking our fellowship. He makes Himself like us; He lives among us; He learns what temptation and suffering are, and He subjects Himself to our hands, becoming our sin, dying so that we may have the opportunity for a relationship with Him. He does this out of His great love of course, but He also does it because our fellowship with Him brings Him great joy and pleasure. God's vulnerability in our relationship is incredible, and He is unashamed to put Himself out on a limb for us, because He knows the incredible joy it brings to both him and us when we turn and pursue Him and seek to be His friend.

Making oneself vulnerable seems a move from a position of weakness when we view it from our human perspective. In fact, to most of us vulnerability is synonymous with weakness. God however makes Himself vulnerable from a position of great strength. His security in Himself, His will, His plans, and His love allow Him to bear his heart to us. Not only this, but it also allows Him to come as close as possible to us in His desire to fellowship with us. He comes right into our very hearts and dwells in a passionate and stubborn temple that prior to His arrival was an idolatrous hot bed of self-worship and human lusts. He resides here and tolerates our lusts and our sins because He knows that victory is already complete, and because there is tremendous joy when He is made Lord and unites with our spirits in fellowship that we have chosen in spite of the fact that our nature desires the contrary so strongly. There is pleasure for God as His presence dwells in this fleshly human temple. A pleasure that we are unable to calculate, and at times are even hard pressed to imagine, could exist from the impurity of our humanity.

    I continue to have a difficult time accepting it, but the wonderful fact is that the center of my Christianity is a relationship with God. This is what I want; it makes me feel good about myself and gives me joy that is infectious to every aspect of my life. I am honored, humbled, and driven by it. It is also what God wants. It pleases Him to have fellowship with us. He enjoys it and delights in our pursuing Him, and the work and sacrifice He has done to set the stage for our relationship is worthwhile from His perspective when we love Him and commune with Him on an intimate level. The joy of our fellowship, companionship, and friendship is the purpose for all creation. An undefiled and sinless relationship with God is the whole purpose of Christ's sacrifice. We are the apple of God's eye, His pride and joy, the objects of His love, just like the children of any good father is to them, only with greater benefits and enjoyment. God craves our fellowship and longs for our friendship. Nothing could be better to have as the center of our Christianity than the relationship that God seeks with each of us.

MY NEW PERSPECTIVE

When I humbly accept that God's great desire is to have fellowship with me, it changes drastically my perspective of Him and me. In our culture God mistakenly is viewed as, *The Great Taker Away of Privileges in the Sky,* and Christianity is viewed as a religion focused on restrictions and strict rules of conduct. This is a gross misrepresentation of our God and our faith brought about by Christians who have something at the center of their Christianity other than a relationship with God. I must admit that I have slipped into this mindset at times, and it has been very detrimental to my faith and my relationship with God. The fact is, God is not nearly as worried about what we don't do, as He is about what we actually do in a positive sense. The restrictions God has placed on us are for our benefit, to keep us from allowing our human nature to run its course and destroy us from the inside out.

God didn't send His only son to die so that we would be mindless automatons who are concerned only with rules for outward actions. He is interested in our hearts and in a relationship that begins there. Although God is in a position of power and authority, and we have offended Him and ruined our initial relationship with Him by our sin, He does not deal with us on the basis of judgment and wrath. These are the alternatives to a relationship with Him, and He is doing all He can to keep us from them. God's motivation for a relationship with us is described in Ephesians chapter one by Paul as His *pleasure*. The same passage states that He chose us, "before the creation of the world (Ephesians 1:4)." These facts continue to describe for us a God who is seeking and pursuing fellowship with His creation. I again have problems accepting the fact that God chose me and that I am made perfect by Christ's blood and God's grace for His good pleasure. The fact is, however, that my intimacy with God pleases Him.

God enjoys me! What an awesome thought. I again have trouble accepting this, but it is true. My relationship with God pleases Him. I was created and chosen by Him for the very purpose of having fellowship with Him. From a human perspective this might be considered a reason to take pride in myself, or feel that I am in a position of power because I possess something that God desires. From a spiritual perspective the exact opposite is true. I am greatly humbled by this dynamic. I feel valued and loved, but also very blessed and fortunate. This new perspective enhances every quality that I love, admire, and respect in God. It also gives me a basis for very positive and appropriate self-esteem.

I know then that God wants a relationship with me, that all His work is for this purpose, and that it pleases, and satisfies Him to fellowship with me. I also know that Christ and His work are at the center of my relationship with God, and all aspects of the relationship are built on Him and His sacrifice. I also know, as I learned with my earthly father, that spending time with God is an important key to building our relationship. What I did not initially know was how to really enhance and grow an intimate relationship with God that is pleasing not just to me, but also to Him. Study, as well as trial and error, led me to three very important factors that have had an important impact on my relationship with God, and are quite evident in the lives of our biblical examples. They are not to replace any type of daily devotional time or corporate fellowship, but I believe are able to enhance them. I have developed a process for myself that includes these three important elements. Actually I didn't develop it; I believe it is evidenced throughout the Bible. These three elements have specific purposes and also are arranged in a specific order. They require time and effort to be attended to properly, and I find it quite difficult to really put myself into them on a daily basis. In fact, I recommend that they are done periodically, with time set aside to allow focus on a relationship with God, using these in a fellowship setting. These elements are isolation, meditation, and communication.

ISOLATION

Spending time alone together is an important factor in building any type of relationship. It is especially important in our relationship with God because we are exposed on a regular basis to so many stimuli that play upon our fleshly desires. Our culture is so saturated with messages that are contradictory to the guiding of the Holy Spirit, that it becomes an absolute necessity for us to periodically cut ourselves off from them so we can *hear* the Spirit's communication more clearly. When I refer to the principle of isolation, I am talking about removing ourselves to a quiet and solitary place where there is no noise and no ability to be distracted. Isolation is the antidote to the persistent bombardment of temptation we experience from living in a cursed and human-controlled world. If we were able to see the full scope of the lives of our Biblical predecessors, I believe we would see frequent periods of time when they isolated themselves and sought God. For many important characters in the scriptures we do see times when they actually lived in isolation, often for long periods. I think it is no coincidence that these periods of isolation often preceded the beginning of their public ministries, or came before the most important events in their lives. For example, Abraham was called out of Ur of the Chaldeans and then later left Haran to wander without peers in a land that was foreign to Him. Moses spent forty years in Midian prior to being spoken to by God and called back to lead his people out of Egypt. Joseph spent years in prison before he was remembered by Pharaoh's cupbearer. David spent his adolescence tending sheep, and was not even present when it was time for his anointing by Samuel. Elijah lived in the wilderness and was fed by the ravens. John the Baptist also lived in isolation near the Jordon, and His entire ministry seems to have taken place away from population centers. Paul discusses, in Galatians chapter one, going into Arabia after his conversion to receive revelation from Christ. These examples appear to outline for us a pattern in the lives of Godly leaders. Isolation, which no doubt included serious seeking and fellowshipping with God, precedes great action and great use by God.

The primary example of the need and use of isolation that we have in Scripture is found in the life of Christ. Immediately after His baptism, Christ is, "Led by the Spirit (Luke 4:1)," into the wilderness to be tempted. He spends forty days secluded from any other human being. Volumes could be written about the time He spent there and the temptations He encountered. Luke's gospel tells us He was continually tempted there during the entire forty days. I personally tend to believe that this was the time during which Christ completely mastered the flesh and prepared Himself for His ministry and His sacrifice. He was also fasting during this period and no doubt spent the majority of this time communing with God, and consuming the spiritual food that would be used to sustain Him over the next three years.

The best scriptural example that I have found for Christ purposely isolating Himself is in Mark 1:35. This verse states, "Very early in the morning, while it was still dark, Jesus got up, left the house and went off to a solitary place, where he prayed." This shows Christ purposely taking time to remove Himself from any distraction and seek God. It was planned and it was at a time and place where His focus would not be interrupted. As I contemplated this verse and began to recognize how important Christ felt it was to be alone with God, so He could maintain His relationship with the Father, I realized that periodic isolation was an absolute must for me if I wanted to develop the kind of relationship that God can enjoy and be pleased with. Throughout the Gospels we see Christ continually removing Himself from the crowds, and towns, and even from His disciples so He could be with God. One of the most meaningful pictures of God in the flesh is when Christ is alone in Gethsemane, struggling with the thought of becoming our sin, and thus being separated from God for the only time in their history. He is alone here again, seeking comfort and strength in the time of His greatest emotional turmoil. From this point His resolve is solidified and He goes on to make the sacrifice for our sin that enables us to have a clean relationship with God.

Our senses are the receptors to our flesh. What we see, hear, feel, smell, and even taste has the potential to feed our selfish and sinful desires. Our senses are taking in information constantly, and the world is preying upon them through the media, advertising, and even interaction with others. Our flesh is fed to some degree just by daily participation in our culture. Isolation is a means for counteracting this process. Freeing ourselves from anything that can prey upon our flesh makes it easier for us to hear and feel the promptings of the Spirit. It opens the door for a distraction-free interaction with God.

I understand the pace and demands that our society has on our time. I am not advocating some sort of medieval monasticism or even a sabbatical. Time alone with God is important to try to have on a daily basis. What I am suggesting is something beyond daily devotionals. Periodically, which may mean weekly, biweekly, or even monthly, it is very important to schedule time when you know you won't be interrupted and you can really focus on your relationship with God. This means an hour or two, or even more, when the cell phones are off and no one can get to you. For some people this may mean going to some place away from their home. This also may mean using a vacation day from work, hiring a sitter for the kids, and maybe even going out of town. I realize this can be difficult to make happen, but God desires it, and we need it. The results will be well worth the effort. Again it is important to recognize that Christ did this quite regularly, and if He felt it was vital to His relationship with God, then it is surely a necessity for ours if we desire the optimum in our fellowship with Him.

MEDITATION

Isolating ourselves periodically is the beginning; it sets the stage for a tightly focused communion with God. Isolation helps free our senses from temptation and distraction. It prepares our bodies and our nature for the spiritual process that will follow. Once our bodies and our physical nature are set, it is important to begin to utilize and focus our minds on enhancing our relationship with God. The primary way to do this is through meditation.

Not to be patronizing to other religions, but for most of my life, when I heard the word meditation, I thought of a guru from some new age or eastern religion sitting with his legs folded, his palms up, and in a trance-like state humming or chanting a specific mantra. This is not at all what I believe the Bible means when it speaks of meditation. The meditation that I am referring to is very much like contemplation and reflection combined. It does not attempt to empty the mind, but to fill it with very specific thoughts, scriptures, or images. Meditation is actually quite an easy thing inside our Christianity because as we focus our minds on spiritual things, the Spirit within us takes our effort and multiplies the results exponentially. As we meditate it actually helps our minds to be transformed from our natural and human instruments of self-indulgence, into a source of Godly thinking patterns. We can use meditation to help us take on and utilize the *mind of Christ*.

I really feel that meditation is something most Christians will find easy to do if they are willing to isolate themselves and focus their minds. Meditation can begin simply with a very specific and narrow thought or image. This may be a sentence from the Bible, an important verse, or an image from Scripture. I feel it is best to keep the volume small and really attempt to work it over in your mind, exploring all the ways that it has, does, and can impact you. When I do this, I consider it, *wrapping my mind around it,* referring to a particular verse or image. You can even meditate on a specific thought that is related to biblical principles. Sometimes a phrase from a song, poem, or book is able to become fuel for meditation. Anything that addresses your relationship with God will work.

Here are some examples of meditations that I have found that are very meaningful and fulfilling for me. They may not be particular items you are interested in using, and you may be far better at using meditation than I am. I am describing them only as examples of types of meditation thoughts. One way I use meditation is by trying to visualize a specific image described in Scripture, one of my favorite passages to use for this is Revelation chapter five. This chapter states:

Then I saw in the right hand of him who sat on the throne a scroll with writing on both sides and sealed with seven seals. And I saw a mighty angel proclaiming in a loud voice, "Who is worthy to break the seals and open the scroll?" But no one in heaven or on earth or under the earth could open the scroll or even look inside it. I wept and wept because no one was found who was worthy to open the scroll or look inside. Then one of the elders said to me, "Do not weep! See, the Lion of the tribe of Judah, the Root of David, has triumphed. He is able to open the scroll and its seven seals.

Then I saw a Lamb, looking as if it had been slain, standing in the center of the throne, encircled by four living creatures and the elders. He had seven horns and seven eyes, which are the seven spirits of God sent out into all the earth. He came and took the scroll from the right hand of him who sat on the throne. And when he had taken it, the four living creatures and the twenty-four elders fell down before the Lamb. Each one had a harp and they were holding golden bowls full of incense, which are the prayers of the saints. And they sang a new song: "You are worthy to take the scroll and to open its seals, because you were slain and with your blood you purchased men for God from every tribe and language and people and nation. You have made them to be a kingdom and priests to serve our God, and they will reign on the earth."

Then I looked and heard the voice of many angels, numbering thousands upon thousands, and ten thousand times ten thousand. They encircled the throne and the living creatures and the elders. In a loud voice they sang: "Worthy is the Lamb, who was slain, to receive power and wealth and wisdom and strength and honor and glory and praise."

Then I heard every creature in heaven and on earth and under the earth and on the sea, and all that is in them singing: "To him who sits on the throne and to the Lamb be praise and honor and glory and power for ever and ever!" The four living creatures said, "Amen," and the elders fell down and worshipped.

I am overwhelmed by this chapter when I begin to meditate on its contents. It gives me a true picture of the uniqueness and divinity of Christ. I am able to catch a glimpse of heaven and God's throne room. I am able to see the twenty-four elders, the four living creatures, and the multitudes of heavenly beings. Even among these, Christ's exceptional attributes distinguish Him and set Him apart from all others. I visualize the power that He has as the *Lion of the Tribe of Judah*, and contrast it with the humble picture of Him as *a lamb looking as if it had been slain*. I begin to contemplate the complexity of my Lord and I am filled with awe, yet my understanding is expanded. I am humbled by my meditation, and yet it encourages me to be strong. My focus is completely on Christ and I begin to develop a deeper appreciation for what He and He alone was and is able to do for me. I enjoy it because it describes my savior in a way that sets Him apart from all others, and gives me hope through the knowledge of His exalted position. It gives me an opportunity to see

Christ in His appropriate setting above all heaven and earth, worshipped and adored by all creation. I allow my mind to pursue any tangent it runs into and when I find one that begins speaking to my heart at that particular time, I tighten my focus on it. I work to visualize the exact seen described in heaven and place myself there with John and the others acknowledging Christ's divinity and worshipping Him as the only worthy opener of the scroll.

This type of visualization helps me to gain an appropriate perspective of God, Christ, and myself. I may not be able to be present in heaven through the Spirit as John was, but I can gain access to the throne room through my meditation. This is why these things were written, to allow us to look more closely into the workings of our God, and join Him there in the intimate fellowship that we both desire. Visualization allows us to make these aspects of God more real and personal. Any passage that is descriptive in this manner can be used for this type of meditation.

Another type of meditation that is very valuable is reflecting on specific scriptures. I sometimes do this on larger passages, but mostly I do it with single verses, or even phrases within a verse. One example is Revelation 13:8 that I mentioned earlier as a verse that ignited the changes in my perspective of my relationship with God. This verse states that Christ was, "The lamb slain at the foundation of the world." I often just focus on this single phrase. I consider the love that God showed for us prior to our species or our world even being created. My mind pours over many of the thoughts that I have already discussed about my relationship with God and His desire to be close to me. Any verse that is meaningful to you in some way can be used for this, especially those that focus on our relationship with God.

The third way that I use to meditate is what I call contemplation. I usually do this when I am outside, often at night. I look at the stars, the moon, or some other aspect of creation and consider how great God is, and how insignificant I seem in comparison to the vastness of His creation. It humbles me, and then I begin to call to mind scriptures, like Genesis chapter twelve where God tells Abraham that his descendants would be like the stars in the sky. I imagine that as one of his spiritual descendants, one of the stars I am gazing at represents me. I remind myself that as beautiful and awesome as the universe and the earth are, that I am the only aspect of creation that was created in God's image and likeness, and that I also am the only part of His creation that He sacrificed His son for. My thoughts continue on this line and they focus once again on my relationship with my creator.

Another very important form of meditation is what I call *altar building*. In the Old Testament when something meaningful happened in the lives of Godly men, they would build altars, sacrifice, and call on the Name of the Lord. I feel that it is very important for us to periodically revisit in our times of meditation the instances in our lives that God saved, comforted, or did something meaningful for us. We may not erect altars of uncut stone or polished bronze to burn the meat of animals on, but something should be done in our hearts to commemorate the workings of God's hand in our lives. These events deserve to be revisited, and they are the anchors that steady us in times of new storms, testifying to God's past faithfulness and holding out hope for His work in the present and the future.

There are a variety of ways to meditate effectively. I have used my own personal methods only as examples, not as a necessary pattern. Visualization, reflection, and contemplation are very useful methods, however. The important thing is for us to fill our minds with thoughts and images that will concentrate on and enhance our relationship with God. Personalizing meditation is the key, what is exciting and meaningful to me personally may or may not be to others. Heavy consideration of our fellowship with God is the key.

COMMUNICATION

I am very fortunate in the sense that as a child my father taught me that praying is like talking to God, and that when I pray I can talk to Him like He were a person present in the room with me. This information was a great gift to me and I began talking to God in that way at a very young age. I was also taught to be very thankful and appreciative when praying and I learned that I could ask God for whatever I wanted. Unfortunately for God and myself, the older I got, the more self-centered my prayer life became. I had no problem asking God for what I wanted, or thought I needed. I wasn't even above begging and pleading and I often would become upset with God when I did not get exactly what I asked for. Communication in my prayer life became a one way street. I thought prayer was supposed to be me talking and God attentively listening. My prayers were more like a shopping list I was dictating to God, than like the real communication with God that He desires.

Later I began to view prayer as one of my means for service. I became very conscious of how much time I was spending in prayer and that the content of my prayers was mostly me asking God to affect some kind of change in people's lives or in our society. I had to work at this type of prayer, but I developed the ability to pray for extended periods often up to or more than an hour at a time. This gave me a sense of accomplishment and even made me feel righteous and productive, but eventually prayer became more like work than like talking to God. It became tedious and ritualistic. The content of my prayer was much less important than the volume. I had inadvertently become like the pagans that Christ described in Matthew 6:7, who ramble on and on to their gods, thinking that quantity is the key to communing with the divine through prayer.

At the same time however, a wonderful thing was happening to me as I studied the Bible. God was using the scriptures to speak right to my life in a very meaningful way. I was being communicated to through His word, and was realizing that interaction with Him was a two-way deal. This was exciting to me, and I couldn't wait to absorb what He was trying to tell me each time I opened up the Bible. I began to spend large volumes of time reading and studying His word, and He blessed me considerably through this. I began to spend more time in the word, and less time in prayer. This dynamic lasted for some time, but eventually reading and studying my Bible also became a burden. I was having a difficult time maintaining the high volume of time I was spending studying, and if I studied for an hour one day, and only forty-five minutes the next, then I felt I'd let God down and my faith and righteousness had gone backwards. I made communication with God something that was not intimate at all, and whether through prayer or reading the Bible, I also made it a ritualistic burden.

As I began to put my relationship with God at the center of my Christianity, my entire perspective and experiences with prayer and Bible study changed. I found that meditating on a small portion of Scripture could be just as valuable to me as hours spent studying. Communication became something that was more intimate and constant. It was prompted by the Spirit and could happen at any time and in any place. It was spontaneous and often times effortless. A wonderful change from the laborious, time- conscious work I had made of it had occurred. I was again talking to God like a father and a friend, just as I did as a child, and just as He desires it.

As I began to isolate and meditate, I also found that something very wonderful developed in my communication with God. Out of my meditation, praise and worship emerged naturally and they reflected the exact feelings of my heart after contemplating and focusing on some aspect of God. No longer were my prayers a wish list to God, centered totally on my needs or desires. They were full of adoration and thanksgiving. They began with thoughts of His holiness and praise for His love and mercy. They were centered completely around Him. Psalm 119:108 says, "Accept, O LORD, the willing praise of my mouth, and teach me your laws," and as I praised Him and worshipped Him I could actually feel that this was occurring, and God's spirit came alive inside of me with joy and satisfaction. These became contagious to my own spirit, and along with them came peace and comfort. As God enjoyed my *sacrifice of praise*, He returned on me blessings that were exponentially greater than what I was pouring out to Him.

Something else happened while I was alone and meditating, God began to speak to my heart while I was seeking Him intensely. The communication aspect of our relationship was being initiated by Him. This was absolutely awesome, and exactly how it is supposed to take place. I found that when I was undistracted, had my mouth shut, and was focused on God, He was able to communicate to me with a closeness and clarity that I had rarely experienced before in my life. For years I communicated with God by asking Him for what I thought I needed, and all of a sudden, God was communicating with me, and giving me exactly what I did need.

Our culture often times makes communication synonymous with self expression, but in reality at least half of the communication process involves listening. As humans, we usually listen and try to develop our responses as we take in information. This again is an example of how poor we are at truly communicating with others. In our relationship with God, He desires communion with Him. He has invited us into a perfect union of the Father, the Son, and the Spirit. The things that they have to express are infinitely more important than what is on my heart and mind, and at times I need to just be silent and listen. If I do, I can soak up the most important mental, emotional, and spiritual answers to all my needs. More importantly, I can get to know God better. He enjoys revealing Himself to me. He wants me to have a deeper knowledge of His mind, His spirit, His will, His power, and His pleasure. When He reveals more of Himself to me I am honored and humbled. I am excited at my new knowledge and the greater depth of our relationship. I feel good about myself and my confidence and self esteem are built up on a very healthy foundation. More importantly, God is blessed. He enjoys revealing more of Himself to us. He is excited when we desire and pursue this. It is fulfilling to Him and He is able to take a wonderful joy out of this type of fellowship with us.

I'm saddened a little when I think of all the things I have missed throughout the years because my mind and mouth were running and God was not able to communicate with me the way He would have liked. Now that I know how sweet communication with Him can be when He initiates it, I am deeply motivated to make sure I take every opportunity to prepare my heart and mind for His words and promptings. Communication that comes from meditation and is initiated by my praise or worship, or by God's speaking to my heart, is the exact kind of fellowship that we were created for, and God enjoys it and is pleased and blessed by it. When we are at this point in our relationship, He is able to look at us as friends, and we receive the blessings and advantages that come with being God's friend.

At times of distress, communication with God is even more important and meaningful in our relationship. The following subsection describes the process of *pouring out hearts out to God*. It describes an honest communication and conveyance of our emotions that is necessary for us to be comforted and consoled by God in our times of deepest emotional turmoil and pain. These instances often are the times when our intimate fellowship with God is most intense and most dear to us and Him.

POURING OUR HEARTS OUT TO GOD

I wish all of my communication with God could be initiated by Him and bring both of us the wonderful and intimate fellowship that we both desire. Unfortunately, my humanness continues to create problems and issues for me that I must deal with that can often negatively affect our relationship, and I have a need to pour the contents of my heart concerning these issues out to God. I am very hesitant about discussing this aspect of communication with God, and I want to be clear that what I am advocating is not intentional disrespect, and in the end it removes barriers that my flesh sets up in our relationship. I am actually advocating complete honesty with God, and He mercifully and graciously accepts this and helps me regain my appropriate perspective of Him and myself when I complete this process.

I really believe that God can do anything He wants. I believe He can rescue me from any kind of trial or temptation. I believe He can answer any prayer I pray, or grant any request that I make. I also know I live on a cursed earth with hurting and wounded people who are going to strike out at me when they feel pain. I also know people are going to make poor decisions that may hurt me or affect me in a negative way. Because of these beliefs about God and my perspective of others, I developed a rather positive characteristic—I don't get easily offended by others and I'm not surprised when people treat me badly. I can let go of anger toward them and usually don't allow them to maintain a place in my thinking process. Most of the time I can even treat them much better than they treat me and even, *turn the other cheek* when necessary. I'm not bragging by making these statements, these qualities are completely contrary to my nature and are a testament to the work of the Spirit in my life. I say these things to set up one very important point about the way my faith and my human thinking patterns collide. Because of my faith in what God can do and my expectations of humans doing negative things, when life is not going the way I hope and expect it to I often times get upset with God. I know this sounds completely blasphemous, but it's the truth. I also get very frustrated with Him, disillusioned, and even angry. Now I'm really sounding bad I know, but it's the truth. Don't get me wrong, I'm not saying that being frustrated with God is right; I'm saying that at times that's what happens to me.

For a relationship of any kind to function properly it must have honesty as one of its standard components. If I said God's ways and His plans never frustrated or upset me, I would be a liar. My heart is still very human in nature, even though it is becoming more like Christ's all the time. The simple fact is, at times I think I know better than God what's best for me, and I get frustrated and angry when He doesn't make my will happen. I begin to develop resentment in my heart toward God. I begin to feel that He is oppressing me or holding me back in some way. I get irritable and bitter just like a child who is not allowed to have something he or she desires. My perspective of God changes when this occurs and I begin to feel that the God of all comfort and freedom is restricting me and that His yoke is too burdensome. This perspective continues as long as I harbor these thoughts in my heart. It only changes when I release them, and I can only release them by verbalizing them to God.

This again sounds horrible, but the truth is God already knows the thoughts in my heart, and they are no more of a sin when I speak them than they are when I store them up. Without giving vent to them they can destroy our relationship, but by speaking them to God I can release them and make room in my heart for His healing and for appropriate thoughts about Him.

In I Peter 5:7, Christ provides for one of the greatest emotional outlets we could ever hope for. Peter says, "Cast your anxieties on him, for he cares for you." God knows every thought and complaint we have, and is big enough to handle whatever we think or say, even if it is something negative about Him. What is intolerable in our relationship is the harboring and feeding of these thoughts. This has the potential to completely destroy our perspective and relationship with God.

There are many Biblical examples of people being frustrated with God and pouring their hearts out to Him. As they do this a wonderful transformation and interaction occurs, and an appropriate perspective is restored. The entire book of Job is a drawn out and intricate picture of this process. Job is frustrated with his circumstances and can't understand how God is working; he even wishes to plead his case before God, but despite this he never leaves the relationship or curses God. He only gives vent to his inner thoughts and feelings. Abraham does the same thing in Genesis chapter fifteen. He is appreciative and humble before God, yet he is frustrated at his lack of a son, even though God has promised him one. He does not hide this, but complains to God, and is reaffirmed by Him after his complaint is heard.

The best examples of the process that I am describing are in the Psalms. In many of these, David vividly pours out his heart to God in questioning laments. His frustration and emotional pain are evident. He lets go of all the questions he has about God that have developed in his heart due to his circumstances. Psalm thirteen has become a very meaningful passage to me. It begins with David asking, "How long, oh Lord? Will you forget me forever?" What a question! Even in my most desperate times when I have been upset with God, I've never thought that God had forgotten me. This sounds almost blasphemous, but it is exactly what was in David's heart, and he loved, respected, and trusted God enough to give voice to it. Like us, he did this not because he had turned his back on God, but because he had no where else to turn, and he knew how mercifully God would listen and accept and heal him.

When we like David begin to pour out our hearts to God, a transformation begins to take place in our flesh. As the bitter and sinful thoughts that we have leave, God does not reject or even punish us, He simply absorbs them, and in

His great mercy and faithful understanding He forgives us. God is not afraid of our questions or our negative feelings, and He is able to endure them in the same manner that He endures all of our sin. He then begins to remind us of His faithfulness. In the past, when I have poured my heart out to God, He has reminded me of all the times that He stood by me when I was enduring trials of various kinds. He also reminds me of facts that I already know, such as the fact that He is the only true source of peace for my life. With my bitter and angry thoughts gone, and with God's loving response filling my heart, my bitterness is ended and the lips that lamented to God now begin to praise Him. Like David in Psalm thirteen, the end of my communication with God has me thanking Him for His unfailing love and praising Him for His gracious mercy.

Great care should be taken in pouring our hearts out to God. It should be done alone and with unlimited time to process with Him. Often times after I have done this, I feel a reaffirmation from God about our relationship, just as Abraham experienced. I realize that He is all I need, and that I want Him more than anything my flesh craves. I also must confess and repent. These end up coming quite naturally when I have emptied myself of all my emotional human garbage. Harboring bitterness toward God is a relationship killer. He can handle any thought or feeling we have about Him, and He wants to help us get rid of them and replace them with thoughts that are true and healthy.

SINNING LESS REVISITED

As I began to focus on putting my relationship with Christ at the very center of my Christianity, I noticed many of the things I had strived for previously began to fall into place with little effort. With relationship at the center, the burden to perform seemed to fade away. I began to realize that Christ's yoke is light because He pulls the vast majority of the load. I also felt the Spirit begin to take more and more control of my life. I still struggle with my flesh, and I still fail at times, but with relationship at the center of my Christianity I am reminded that God's grace is big, that confession brings about immediate forgiveness, and that my standing with God is not something that is shifting. My position with God is static. I have been blessed with every spiritual blessing in Christ, and seated with Him at God's right hand Paul tells me in Ephesians chapter one. My sin inside of grace does not change this fact or move me in and out of my blessed position. When I consider these facts my thankfulness overflows and I am awed by God's great mercy and love for me.

When focused on my relationship with God I find that

I sin less simply because my desire to sin is not as prominent. The principal of *replacement* was naturally occurring in my life. By this I mean that as one element leaves, another must come to replace it, or as one element becomes more prominent, its opposite must decline. In a spiritual sense the two elements that are vying for control of my life are my flesh and God's spirit. They are in a zero-sum game within my heart and mind. Wherever one gains some ground in a part of my life, the other loses ground. Amazingly this is the fight I was unable to win when I attempted to put sinning less at the center of my Christianity. I could not win it from that perspective because I was using my own human ability to try and fight sin. Essentially I was using my flesh to fight my flesh, and there was no way I could make a lasting change by this means.

As I put my relationship with Christ in its proper place, I began to sin less. Many of the sins I listed and attempted to eradicate by my own will, without lasting success, began to fade from and even leave my life. Temptations in many areas began to subside or be less intense. There was still that struggle with the flesh that we never escape in this life, but I felt better about it than I ever had. I again stumbled onto a verse that I had known for years that took on a whole new meaning with my relationship at the center of my Christianity. I had even memorized it in the past; Romans 8:13 says, "If by the Spirit you put to death the misdeeds of the body, you shall live."

"By the Spirit," was a phrase I began to contemplate closely, trying to understand just what that verse meant. I realized that in my life, if I fed the Spirit and it took more and more control of my life that it would choke out the sin in my life. John 3:34 tells us that God gives the Spirit without limit, but God's spirit, like Him, is not pushy or forceful with us. Even though we have the Spirit living inside of us, He refuses to dominate or bully us. I have come to the realization that the one thing that truly limits the Spirit's work in my life is me. I have a distinct choice, I can feed the flesh and allow it to dominate my life and thinking patterns, or I can feed the Spirit and allow it to control my life and perspective. I found that if I put effort into my relationship with God and fruitfully isolated, meditated, and communicated with Him, the Spirit was fueled, and it became more and more prominent in all aspects of my life. It takes over my thinking patterns and I am able to access its wisdom, understanding, insight, guidance, comfort, peace, and all the other qualities that it possesses and that I need.

Another wonderful thing begins to happen, my sinful desires begin to diminish. Temptations become easier to resist, and some things that used to tempt me are no longer appealing to me at all. Increased influence of the Spirit and sinning less are byproducts of a healthy relationship with God. I was accomplishing one of my goals without even working on it directly.

SERVICE REVISITED

With relationship at the center of my Christianity, service takes on an all new light. I still believe that obedience and faithfulness in service are of extreme importance. God created work for several reasons and work does some things for our self esteem and our self image that are very vital, and are very difficult to replace with anything else. God has a will and plans that we fit into, and we play an integral part in making them come to fruition. It is very easy for me to perceive myself as a servant or a slave to Christ. I'd stay in this role nearly all the time if that is what I believed He wanted. I also know that He'll have work for us in eternity and it will also be very rewarding and fulfilling, and unlike now, always quite productive, but even then the master-servant role will not dominate our relationship. I'd be happy for it to, both now and then, but that's not what God wants and it's not why He created us.

The fact that I am God's child and perhaps even His friend does not make me want to serve Him less. In fact, it makes me want to serve Him more. My human nature still carries a desire to try and pay God back for what he has done for me. God however, is not interested in paybacks. Remember, He has done so much for us because it pleases Him and He wants a relationship with us. God appreciates our work and our effort, but we sometimes seem to think that He'll love us more if we do more for Him. The truth is He can't demonstrate His love in any greater way than He already has. Working may make us feel better about our position with God, but it doesn't change that position.

Ephesians 2:10 is a verse that has been a great motivating force in my life and has even haunted me at times. It states that we are, "God's workmanship, created in Christ to do good works, which God prepared in advance for us to do." I lived in fear that I would not accomplish all the good works God prepared in advance for me, and that I would let Him and others down. A verse meant for encouragement turned into an idea that carried great anxiety. I was creating a burden God never intended and my motivation was both obligation and fear, and these are not the motivations of someone in a loving and fulfilling relationship. As a result I began to hunt and even invent jobs that I thought Christ needed done or would be happy seeing me do.

With relationship at the center of my Christianity my service began to change. It became more natural and less pressured, and often times less planned. Opportunities opened when I was ready for them, and I merely stepped in and let God work. I discovered one of the most important principles established about service; God can do more *through* me than I can do *for* Him. I have talents and abilities, I know my strengths, and I try to use them for Christ. I Peter 4:10 tells

The Road to Relationship

us that we all have gifts and we should all use them, but if I am the single guide behind the use of my gifts, then they are not being used as they were designed. In fact, there are times that my actions, even with pure motives, can impede God's work. Sometimes I need to just get out of God's way and let Him perform what He wants through me. If I am in control of all the work I do for Christ, then I will never truly know if His will is being served, I'm only doing what I guess He wants. I have found the most productive I can be for Christ, is when I feel as though I am merely a conductor, and God's power is flowing through me to others freely, uninhibited by the regulation of my mind, will, or spirit.

In John chapter fifteen Christ said that if we remain in Him, and He in us, we will produce good fruit. For years I thought that part of my duty as a Christian was to search out good deeds or jobs that God had for me to do. I often felt these were somewhat hidden, and if I didn't stay vigilant, I might miss the most important jobs I was designed for, and I might even miss the very purpose for which I was put on this earth. My perspective was completely shattered as God worked on my heart through various scriptures.

Abraham has always been a very important character to me in my times of Bible study. He is the prototype for a relationship with God. Chosen from among all men, he is the father of our faith, and outside of Christ I believe he is probably the most important figure in the Bible. As I studied his life, I found that service was not a primary focus of his relationship with God. God gave him only a few commands, the primary one found in Genesis 17:1 stating, "Walk before me and be blameless." He had no written code or even a divine revelation of what was right and wrong, and though he made sacrifices to God there was very little instruction as to how he was to sacrifice and virtually no ceremony or ritual that went with it. It seems so simplistic, but Abraham merely believed God, and acted according to what God had told him. He wasn't perfect, he made mistakes, he tried to manipulate God's plan by human means, and he struggled to rationalize the impossible promise God gave him with his own human thought processes. What makes Abraham great is that he never returned to his former life and he struggled through twenty-five years of relative silence without relinquishing hope. The relationship he had with God was founded on a promise and fueled by faith, and the strict service that we often feel is necessary to please God was distinctly absent. However, when God did call Abraham to action, because of their relationship, he acted without hesitation or question in offering his son Isaac in Genesis chapter 23.

We venerate Abraham for his unhesitating obedience to God's command to sacrifice his son. This is one of the greatest acts of faith in the entire Bible. Abraham was willing not because of his years of service as a Sunday school superintendent, or as a deacon, or an evangelist, or because of any position or service he had or did at all. He acted in such a way because he had nearly four decades of relationship with God, and God had proven Himself faithful over and over again in Abraham's life. Abraham was not chosen because of his service or even because of his righteousness, his family were idolaters in Ur of the Chaldeans. God's choice of jobs and servants is based on His own reasons, not all of which we see. The best and most productive service comes from a

The Road to Relationship

healthy relationship with Him, is initiated by Him, and will be made known clearly to us by Him.

God's precedent is to interrupt the lives of faithful men and women with the work that He has for them to do. He doesn't hide our jobs or good deeds, and He doesn't require us to search and search until we find our purpose. Serving God requires very little on our part. We must fuel our relationship with Him first and foremost—all productive service stems from this. After this we simply must be obedient and faithful on a daily basis, and when opportunity arises, willing to step into it.

There are dozens of Biblical examples of God working this way. One of the best is in Acts chapter three. Peter and John healed the man born crippled and it became a great witness to the people of Jerusalem. They had no intention of doing this. It wasn't planned or thought out in advance. They were simply going to the temple at the hour of prayer, being obedient and faithful in their relationship with Christ. This is the context in which God is able to work the most successfully and thoroughly. God interjects service into healthy relationships that He has with His children. Relationship opens the door for and provides the motivation for service. God provided the opportunity, and they acted under the guidance of the Spirit and in the timing that God had planned. This is why the results of their actions were so productive, and as a result the church in Jerusalem was galvanized and grew in number.

God works in our lives in the same way. As our relationship with Him grows, so do all the other characteristics that a good servant needs. Our obedience, willingness, insight, love, faithfulness, and whatever else God needs in us is produced as a result of our fellowship with Him. When the times are right God opens the door for us to use our gifts and talents in a way He has planned. It can be as simple as offering a cup of water in His name Jesus said, or as complex as administering some type of Christian organization. God won't let us miss what He has planned for us, and it will most likely be things that are much greater than we would have planned ourselves. Our dreams are so small, but we will be limited to them if we are the motivation and energy behind them. God's plans are so large that we often shy away from them, or doubt our ability to carry them out. That's fine, so did Moses, Gideon, Jeremiah, and most others He called. We must remember however, that the work God does is planned, guided, and fueled by Him, He only needs human conductors who are willing to step into them and be used by Him. If we feel inadequate, it's because we are, but thankfully we aren't the source of power that accomplishes the service of God.

TRIALS REVISITED

In my work as a therapist I daily encounter patients who are depressed, bipolar, have extensive abuse histories, have auditory or visual hallucinations, or a variety of other mental health issues. I am honest with them and tell them that I don't really understand what it is like to be in their position. I have studied their issues and worked with people who have similar conditions as my patients, but I have not experienced them firsthand, therefore, even though I have some understanding of their issues I don't have an experienced-based perspective of them. I can be empathetic and compassionate with them. I often even have knowledge that can help them, but I can't say that I fully understand what they are going through. Unlike my professional relationship with my patients, Christ knows intimately what it is like to experience and feel exactly what I am going through at any moment because He has experienced it in the flesh.

As I look at trials from a relationship perspective this fact becomes very dear to me. I am acutely aware of what my flesh and human nature is like. I understand how it is contrary to all that God wants and I know that left to my own devices, my flesh will destroy me. I know the terrible, vindictive, lustful, greedy, and angry thoughts that have lived inside of me, and how my flesh pursues these and is fed by them. I know how powerful and selfish it is and how it can consume my entire thought process. I know how vile it is at my very core. I know what it is like to hurt and to be hurt, to have emotional pain that lingers months and years and dogs my every thought. I know what it is like to be frustrated, betrayed, and taken advantage of by others. I know how weak my fleshly heart can be and how it can be broken and sorrowful. I know well all the negative aspects of my fleshly human nature and I despise it. I hate it and I want to see it destroyed by the Spirit that lives within me. I want to leave it behind and rid myself of all its faults and desires, but Christ my Lord willingly clothed Himself in this horrible humanness for us so that He could understand us better, mediate perfectly between God and us, and so He could take on all of our sin and destroy it with His human body on the cross. He pursued the taking on of what I so badly want to get rid of, and experienced all the things I hate and despise so that He could intimately understand us from a human perspective. I love Him dearly for this.

 I'm human and I hate my own flesh, I can't imagine what it would feel like to be God and have to endure this sinful nature. James chapter one tells us that God does not tempt, nor can He be tempted. This means that God didn't even know what we felt like or the struggle we experience when we are tempted until Christ experienced those same temptations in the flesh. There is nothing more dear or central to my faith than Christ's sacrifice, but the fact that He endured this flesh I hate so much, and that He has an intimate understanding of what it is like to be human endears Him to me. There is no trial, or test, or temptation I can encounter that He did not experience and triumph over. When I seek Him in my time of need I know that He has been right where I am, and He sympathizes with my weakness. This is so wonderfully described in Hebrews 4:14–16,

> Therefore, since we have a great high priest who has gone through the heavens, Jesus the Son of God, let us hold firmly to the faith we profess. For we do not have a high priest who is unable to sympathize with our weaknesses, but we have one who has been tempted in every way, just as we are—yet was without sin. Let us then approach the throne of grace with confidence, so that we may receive mercy and find grace to help us in our time of need.

Christ has every opportunity to gloat or condemn when I am suffering because He endured such things without sin, and He knows that I am powerless to save myself. He does the exact opposite however, by sympathizing with me and inviting me to the throne where He now resides and offers me mercy and grace sufficient enough to meet the needs that I come to Him with. He understands the mental, emotional, spiritual, and physical stress that we endure, and he can relate to it and advocate to the Father for us. Hebrews beautifully describes Christ in His role as our perfect High Priest, the only true mediator between God and man, able to fulfill this role because He is God and He has been flesh. He understands completely the Holy perfection of divinity and the utter weakness of our human nature. Christ's work did not end on the cross. He is not inactive at the Father's right hand waiting for His kingdom to come. His work as the mediating High Priest is constant. These facts completely change my perspective when I consider my trials in the light of my relationship with God. I know when I cry for help in the midst of my pain, Christ sits at God's right hand and has access to His right ear. From this position He pleads to the father on my behalf. I often imagine the conversation they have and I suppose that Christ's part of the dialogue sounds something like this:

> Father, bear with my brother, Andy, I know what it is like to suffer in the way that he is currently experiencing. I know how close I came to giving into the flesh and how easily the human heart fails. The pressure is so difficult to bear, Father. In the flesh my mind was such a battlefield. He is confused now and needs the clarity of your Spirit. Even if he fails, Daddy, don't condemn him, remember that he is why I was chosen and I have paid the price for whatever sin he might commit. The pain that exists in the hearts of man is strong, and it affects the reasoning of the human mind. I struggled with that pain when I was in his place. Whatever he does, Father, remember that he loves you, and that my blood has redeemed him for your pleasure. Lavish him with the blessings that my blood has acquired. Pour your grace out to him, Father, and be merciful to him. Be patient with him

The Road to Relationship

and bear with him regardless of what he does. He is the reason I left you, Father, he is why you sent me. Make our Spirit a fire in him and help him conquer the flesh. Protect and guard my brother, Father. He loves you so much, and the pain and temptation he is enduring is so frustrating. Listen to him as he cries out to you and have mercy on him.

I believe this type of exchange happens on all our behalves perpetually, and it gives me courage and strength to face whatever this life presents me. God now knows intimately how it feels to be in my position, and He wants to comfort me and make me successful. With this in mind I can persevere and grow regardless of my circumstances, and I am able to take solace in the fact that no matter what trial I encounter, God is faithful and He is using it to enhance the relationship He and I have. Though great pain may be present in my flesh, deeper intimacy and fellowship are occurring within our relationship.

SELF-IMAGE WITHIN OUR RELATIONSHIP

Self-image and self-esteem are topics I have rarely heard taught in Christian circles, but how we feel about ourselves is a very important part of how we view God, have a relationship with Him, and how we treat others. As I discussed before, I was acutely aware of my sin and how it separated me from God, even at a young age. I grew up to hate sin and I despise it in my own life more than in any other context. It is very easy for me to continue to view myself primarily as a lowly sinner, saved and accepted only because of God's grace and mercy. This is true, but in actuality we are much more than this. II Corinthians 5:17 tells us that we are *new creations* in Christ and that, "The old has gone and the new has come." Through Christ we are able to feel very good about ourselves in light of our relationship with God. In fact, God probably looks at us in a much more favorable light than we view ourselves. Remember that when He sees us, He sees no sin. Nothing stands in the way of Him viewing us as sin-free new creatures.

This perspective does not contradict biblical humility,

but embraces it. I grew up thinking that humility meant thinking negatively about myself, but this is not at all what God desires. Humility is understanding that God is pure, and holy, and sovereign, and that I am His creation made for His glory and pleasure. To be humble is to acknowledge that all I have has been given to me by God, not to feel that I am worthless or devoid of value. The opposite of this is actually true. God placed incredible value on us when He determined that the price for our salvation would be His one and only son. We are actually the most valuable things in all creation because of the high price of our redemption. All the rest of God's creation on earth will be renewed and cleansed by fire II Peter chapter three tells us, but it took the death of His son to return us to perfection.

God wants us to understand our value and live and act accordingly. It is a fact of human nature that we will live and act more productively if we feel good about ourselves and our position with God, rather than feeling negatively or poorly about ourselves or our relationship with Him. The fact that God loves us and is intimately interested in us is very humbling. If He cares so much about us, then He surely expects that we should care about ourselves and take joy in the fact that He desires our fellowship. There are four biblical facts that we should base our self-image and self-esteem on. They outline for us the perspective God has of us and the appropriate way in which we should view ourselves from within the relationship we have with Him.

The first fact is found in Genesis 1:27; we are told that we are made in God's own image and likeness. As I have stated before, this is a unique fact that separates us and sets us above

The Road to Relationship

all other aspects of God's creation. All aspects of creation apart from man come solely from the limitless imagination of God. God's creative ability is almost inconceivable to us in our current fleshly state, and His creation is so vast, complicated, diverse, and awesome that we can become very intimidated when viewing ourselves in context with the entire universe. The wonderful fact about God's creation is that man is the only aspect of it in which He used a pattern—Himself. It is true that we possess a rebellious and sinful nature, but God created man in glorious perfection to inhabit and rule over all the earth. He gave us a complex mind that is able to understand and discern both wisdom and knowledge that He is the source of. He gave us a heart that experiences emotions, just as He does. He also made us vessels that are able to house His spirit, and His great desire is to come and live in us and fellowship with us. We are innately sinful and prone to evil, but despite this fact, we are still more like God than any other aspect of His creation, and in eternity—when we are finally free of sin—this glorious aspect of our creation will be fully revealed to us.

The second fact is that God paid a high price for our redemption. He of course sent His son for us. The price of our salvation is incalculable to us now because we currently do not truly understand the heights at which Christ existed prior to coming to earth in fleshly form. Someday this will be revealed to us and we will be both amazed and completely thankful for the sacrifice He made. I Peter 2:24 says, "He bore our sins in His body," and II Corinthians 5:21 says, "God made him who had no sin to be sin for us." The dreaded price that Christ paid was not merely physical, but also spiritual. From eternity past to all eternity that exists in the future, God and Christ have had a perfect relationship. The only point that this relationship was ever broken was when Christ became our sin on the cross, and God was forced to forsake Him. That is the price paid for the restoration of our relationship with God. The fact that both considered this an act that they were willing to endure sheds light on their view of the importance of restoring our relationship with them. It also should be very positive fuel for our self- image.

The third fact is that God has a purpose for each of us. I have discussed Ephesians 2:10 and I Peter 4:10 previously. They tell us that God has prepared good works for us, and that He has given each of us gifts to use in administering His grace. God wants to use us to accomplish His will and His plans. In fact, we are vital to the fulfillment of His plans and the fullness of His body, the church. God feels that we are important enough to partner with in accomplishing His goals. He also gives us the power and wisdom to do His work by leaving for us the Holy Spirit. The Spirit resides in us and comforts, encourages, and guides us. We are not dependent upon our own resources to do the Lord's work. He is with us every step of the way, compensating for our human weakness and inadequacies. God has given us a trust; He has left us with His word, His spirit, and His work. He believes in us and wants to use us on a daily basis. This should make us truly feel like the chosen people that he continually tells us that we are.

The fourth fact is that Christ is returning for us. In John 14:1–4 Christ tells His disciples that He is going to prepare a place for them and because of this fact, He will return for them. God's promise holds true for us also. Christ is preparing a place for each of us and He is going to dwell with us for all eternity. When I consider that I will spend eternity with God, I always view this as one of the great goals of my faith, but it is also one of God's great desires. I'm impacted when I consider the fact that Christ Himself is preparing a place for me. He is at work crafting my reward. It's a work He has chosen to do Himself because of His great love for us. If Christ's desire is to return for me and to live with me forever, then I should be able to see value in myself and feel good about myself because of the way He views and treats me.

These four facts: I am made in God's image and likeness, God sent His son to restore our relationship through His death, God has a purpose for me, and Christ is returning for me, should be the foundation of our self-image. These do not contradict the principle of biblical humility, but when viewed in the appropriate context they should embrace it. It is humbling to know how much God cares and works for us. If His perspective of us is so positive and encouraging, then surely we should feel the same way about ourselves. We are creatures of great value, unequalled by any other part of creation, and God wants us to take joy and receive peace from this fact. Having a positive self-image also makes us able to relate to others in a more loving and godly way. Being secure in these facts helps us drive out envy, jealousy, selfish ambition, and a need to seek affirmation in ungodly ways. These facts are unchanging. Regardless of what might happen in my life, good or bad, I can always count on these four facts being true and intact. If I build my self-esteem on anything else, then its foundation is open to change. My talents, accomplishments, looks, intelligence, or money are all subject to change, and often do throughout life. If my self-image is based on them, or even on how others feel about me, or the relationships I have with them, then my self image is never stable. My self-esteem will be like a roller coaster with great highs and great lows that are dependent upon the various circumstances of my life. If I am anchored to these four facts however, I can be secure and even confident regardless of how others treat me and despite what might happen to me. This is a priceless gift that God has given me in a world of inconsistency and persistent change. It also insures that I will be able to uphold my end of my relationship with Him in a healthy and productive manner. God did not make us for a relationship in which we feel poorly about ourselves. If this were the case, we would eventually feel negatively about the one who created us. He wants us to live out our relationship with Him from the same perspective that He has of us, which is overwhelmingly positive.

MY CIRCUMSTANCES DO NOT DEFINE OUR RELATIONSHIP

Humans have an innate need to attach themselves to something greater than themselves. If they do not do this, then they are forever involved in activities of self pursuit. Being associated with something larger than ourselves gives us a sense of importance, value, identity, and safety. Those of us who have attached ourselves to and have a relationship with Christ have found the appropriate entity that provides for all our identity needs, but we often continue to fight being identified with or defined by other factors in our lives. The most common factors that people use to define themselves are socioeconomic status, occupation, race or ethnicity, education level, and family. Many of these can be determined about someone merely by observing them or carrying on a short conversation with them. We often use exploratory questions to make such defining determinations such as, "What do you do for a living," or "Do you have a family?" Defining ourselves and others in various ways is common to all civilizations and cultures, and has been throughout human history.

Many times we experience different types of circumstances that are greater than ourselves. When this happens we often tend to define ourselves and our relationship to God by these circumstances. For example, many people who find out they have cancer immediately define themselves as *cancer patients*. This may continue throughout the duration of their illness, and if they are healed of their disease they then begin to view themselves as *cancer survivors*. People who have been robbed or oppressed in some way have the tendency to view themselves as victims. There are many other circumstances that have the power to consume the human perspective and lead us to define ourselves and our outlook by them. Divorce, death, job loss, and even positive things like promotions and degrees have this ability. We also allow these circumstances to dictate how we feel or think about our relationship with Christ.

The world and our flesh also like to categorize us by what we possess or achieve. The "American Dream" is characterized by wealth and materialism, fame and popularity. The rich and famous are painted by our culture as holding the ideal position in our society. This leaves the vast majority of us feeling as though we are on the outside looking in. We begin to define ourselves by what we don't have instead of what we do possess. This leaves us with even greater desires to look beautiful, be in shape, have money, live in luxury, or at least have what the neighbors down the street have. In the richest nation on earth, our culture is continually feeling as though they need more. The media in turn fuels this feeling. Madison Avenue is built on feelings of inadequacy and the desire for more that plagues our collective thinking process. Our national ideal has become a materialistic mirage that is unattainable and only devours those who pursue it.

The Road to Relationship

As a Christian there is absolutely nothing that defines me as distinctively as being chosen and redeemed by God, and having His Holy Spirit living inside of me, and being involved in a growing relationship with Him. All other characteristics and circumstances that exist in my life are temporary. Everything is secondary to my relationship with Christ. His presence in my life defines me. He is greater than any circumstance or situation that I may ever find myself in. He is the giver of all I possess and the source that can supply anything that I need.

Who I am as a Christian is a constant. Who I am as a Christian is defined by what is going on inside of me. My identity should be taken over by Christ. He is who I am trying to become like. He is who should be spilling out of me. Outside circumstances don't define who I am; they give God a chance to reveal Himself more in me, and more through me. When I am in difficult circumstances I draw closer to God and others notice it. Circumstances don't define *who* I am; they reveal *whose* I am. If circumstances defined us, then Jesus was a crazy man whose own family wanted to take Him away from His public ministry, and the apostle Paul was a jailbird who was constantly causing civil unrest wherever he went. We know however, that Jesus was Son and Savior before He ever came to earth, and Paul was an apostle and evangelist no matter where his physical body was at. Christ living in us is greater than anything we can ever encounter, outside forces don't shape Him, He has control over them. They are His tool for His purpose and glory, to help us let go of our identity and take on His. Our relationship with Him is at the center of who we are.

If we allow circumstances to define us, we are not being truthful about the God who lives inside of us. He is eternal and whatever circumstance we are in will not last forever. The world is defined by their circumstances and because of this they lead a life of drastic emotional ebbs and flows. There is nothing at their core that is constant from which they can draw strength. Our relationship with God is greater than anything we will ever experience and it is able to supercede anything we encounter, giving us peace when we should feel despair, and strength when we appear utterly weak.

THE DECEITFULNESS OF OUR EMOTIONS

Our emotions are part of what makes us like God. Having and experiencing emotions is an example of how we are made in God's image and likeness. There are numerous places in Scripture where God expresses hate. One of these is Psalm 101:3, which states, "The deeds of faithless men I hate." Genesis 6:6 states, "The LORD was grieved that he had made man on the earth, and his heart was filled with pain." This verse plainly shows that God experiences emotions we are familiar with. I also feel that there are few places in Scripture that better demonstrate God's possession of emotion more than Mathew 23:37–39 which states,

> O Jerusalem, Jerusalem, you who kill the prophets and stone those sent to you, how often I have longed to gather your children together, as a hen gathers her chicks under her wings, but you were not willing. Look, your house is left to you desolate. For I tell you, you will not see me again until you say, "Blessed is he who comes in the name of the LORD."

Here we see the expression of centuries of a longing and sorrowful heart that desires only comfort and peace for His persistently disobedient people. God's emotions, like Him, are pure, honest, and perfect—felt and expressed in the most perfect way. However, our emotions are seated in our human hearts and subject to the passions of our sinful nature. Remember, Jeremiah 17:9 tells us that the human heart is, "Deceitful above all things and beyond cure." Because our emotions are so tied to our human nature they very often end up being a hindrance to our spiritual growth process. This usually happens because they cloud our view of spiritual reality. How I feel is often quite contrary to the spiritual facts about my life. My feelings and emotions quite often lie to and attempt to deceive me.

One of the flaws of our human nature is that we often base our decision making on how we feel. We also tend to base our beliefs about our world and ourselves on how we feel. We function on the precept that if we feel something then it must be true. This is called *emotional reasoning*, and it is a very critical thinking error that can plague our lives and our Christianity. Discerning between our human emotions and the promptings of the Holy Spirit can be very tricky because the Holy Spirit also tends speak to us through feelings or a communication in our spirit that cannot be defined as just a thought. Understanding the difference between the feelings produced by our emotions and the spiritual reality that we live in and that is testified to by the Spirit, is of extreme importance in our relationship with God.

Paul outlines the difference between our emotions and the spiritual reality that we live in, in II Corinthians 4:7–12. In these verses he states that we are hard pressed but not crushed, perplexed but not in despair, persecuted but not abandoned, and struck down but not destroyed. The Corinthians, as well as many of us at one time or another, probably felt that they were crushed, in despair, abandoned, or destroyed. These are the human emotions that often occur when we experience stress or trials. The spiritual reality however, is that they—and we in turn—are not crushed, in despair, abandoned, or destroyed. Our relationship with Christ and the Holy Spirit living inside of us will not permit us to live in these states. We may feel we are, but that is not the case. In stressful situations our flesh and the Spirit often engage in a battle for our minds to attempt to influence our decision making. We have two distinct choices: to act on what the human elements of our hearts feel or on what we believe is the spiritual reality of our situation. Here is the point where real faith is both built and expressed. Regardless of my feelings, I am never completely crushed, in despair, abandoned, or destroyed, and I can live and act according to my true spiritual position. These facts may not take away the stress or pain, the fact is, I am at times hard pressed, perplexed, persecuted, and struck down. However, when I am focused on the reality that God is in control of my circumstances and He will not allow me to experience the full consequences they can bring to the human heart, I am able to receive what He wants to generously give me. He gives strength instead of allowing me to be crushed, hope instead of despair, comfort instead of abandonment, and life instead of destruction, turning each of the intended curses into a blessing I can only experience and appreciate when I am at the end of my flesh. Those without Christ do not get these divine benefits in times of trials. They are subject to being crushed, in despair, abandonment, and even emotional destruction. We may experience difficult emotions, but we have the promise that our position will never be devastating—it is secure and safe—and we are able to take great comfort and joy in this fact. God takes us right to the edge of our human limitations and then pushes us past them, allowing us to see how inadequate and dependent upon Him we are. He then stretches out His merciful hand and saves us from complete despair and destruction. He then lovingly asks at this point, "Do you know how really good I am now?" We thankfully answer, "Yes;" and He replies, "No you don't, but you're starting to get a clue."

Our love for God grows here because we see more clearly the extent to which He has saved us from ourselves, our sin, our desires, and our world that is run by the common human delusion that we can make the best decisions for our own lives. We will never fully know how good God is until we leave this life and are finally free of the fleshly influence on our view of spiritual matters, but we can begin to appreciate the love and mercy that are the motivation in God's stripping away of our flesh. Because of this, our hope increases, we pursue God more wholeheartedly, and our relationship with Him is able to move to new levels of fulfillment for us and enjoyment for Him. We begin to see with spiritual eyes and insight, the deceit of our emotions becomes apparent to us, we forget about the pain that accompanies the death of our flesh, and we are able to worship God in spirit and truth.

To the human perspective this may sound foolish, but God's allowing us to experience difficult times that stretch us emotionally is actually an act of great mercy. He takes us right to the edge of the chasm that contains the darkest depths of human emotions. He allows us to look into it and see feelings of being crushed, despair, abandonment, and destruction, but He is unwilling to let us fall in and experience these. We may feel them, but the reality is that we do not *experience* them. From the edge of the chasm, God's comforting Spirit draws us back to a safe place and reminds us how frail we are and how dependent we are upon Him. The Spirit stands vigil day and night at the edge of the chasm and protects us from the harm that lies at its bottom. He compensates for the weakness of our emotions, and as we submit to Him He provides strength for all that we must endure and accomplish in such situations. We are often able to see God work most effectively when we are at our emotional end, and our faith grows as we are forced to rely on Him. It is frightening to stand at the edge of that chasm, but only there can we fully understand how God continually saves us from the weaknesses of our own human nature. Only there are we able to acknowledge the depth of His comfort and mercy, and begin to lose our love and dependence upon our flesh, from there we see with eyes of truth unhindered by our deceitful emotions.

God also compensates for the weakness of our emotions by delivering His truth straight to our hearts. When our flesh is failing and the things we see, hear, and feel are all leading us into a state of fear or hopelessness, the Spirit steps in and returns us to the proper perspective. Paul describes this process in Romans 8:15–16, stating that the Spirit we have received leads us out of the bondage to fear that our human natures once lived in, He testifies with our spirits that we are God's children, and He then reminds us that God knows how to take care of His kids. Even when we are consumed by our own sin and guilt, God does not allow this to stand in the way of what He wants to give us. I John 3:19–22 tells us that when our hearts are not at rest in his presence and in turmoil over our guilt and our inadequacies, He is greater than our hearts and puts them at rest in His presence allowing us to approach Him with confidence. The ability to approach God with confidence is also attested to in Hebrews 4:14–16, previously discussed, and it is a gift that will never be completely appreciated until we see God in all his perfection and unique holiness.

The wonderful thing about being able to approach God in this way is that He desires to give us the things we seek. He is a loving daddy who wants to take away the hurts of His kids and replace them with peace and joy. We have to encounter turmoil in our flesh because if we do not, we tend not to seek Him as desperately as we do when we are hurt. God uses pain, whether mental, physical, or emotional, to remind us that this world our flesh loves is actually a miserable and horrible place corrupted by our sin. If we aren't reminded by this fact, we tend to become very comfortable here and enjoy the temporary things that are so greatly inferior to the lasting experiences we have in our relationship with God. It is a terribly wonderful thing to be at the end of our flesh. We hate it and rebel against it. We despise the pain and we strike out in bitter reaction to it, but only when we reach the end of our flesh are we able to see God work in His most successful, loving, merciful, and complete way. It is at this point that Paul is able to say in I Corinthians 12, that when he is weak, then he is strong, because here Christ is working unimpeded by our nature, and from that position His unlimited strength can be expressed through our mortal minds and bodies. Paul precedes this statement in chapter twelve with all his sufferings in chapter eleven. He is telling us that the power Christ exacts through him is a direct result of the death of his flesh created by his suffering. Paul is able to glory in suffering and weakness because at this point in his life, he is able understand and appreciate how God has used it to grow their relationship and further His purpose in Paul's life and ministry. It is a fearful thought to me, but it seems that greatness in Christ and true appreciation of His love and mercy is preceded by suffering because it provides a context through which we can see how deceitful our emotions can be by taking on the mind of Christ. This horrible position to our flesh is the place from which Christ can achieve the most in our lives, and from which we can learn the most about Him and grow the most dramatically in our faith. We understand what truth is and we are free from the deceitfulness and utter weakness of our human emotions. The distinction between spiritual reality and what our human hearts believe to be true is clearly seen at the end of our flesh. At this point I am thankful for what God has given me, for what He is continually freeing from my human weaknesses, and the fear that has plagued us ever since Adam and Eve hid from the Lord in the shame of their nakedness.

MY NEED FOR SELF EXPRESSION

There is a uniqueness and individuality that is divinely placed in the spirits of all humans. Despite heredity and regardless of environment, each of us is singularly crafted by the hand of the Father. Jeremiah 1:5 states, "Before I formed you in the womb I knew you, before you were born I set you apart; I appointed you as a prophet to the nations." This obviously shows that before God formed Jeremiah in the womb He *knew* him, and set him apart as a prophet. Life does not begin at birth, or even at conception, but in the heart and mind of God. Humans have a general desire to fit in to social groups and to be accepted by others, but we also have a need to be seen and judged as individuals. There is a voice inside each of us that longs to be heard and to express to the world our thoughts and dreams and opinions. We have an innate drive that leads to self expression. We even admire self expression in art, music, literature, sports, politics, and a variety of other areas. The ability to conceptualize and relay information to others is part of what makes us different from all other forms of creation.

I have found that my desire for self expression is tied very closely to my human emotions. I most frequently want to express myself when I am angry, frustrated, happy, excited, annoyed, or anxious. I also find there is frequently a need to express myself when I feel insecure or require some type of affirmation. Because my self expressive tendencies are so tied to my human nature, I often find that my desire for expression is at odds with my Christianity and detrimental to my relationship with God. This point is most notably proven by the fact that I often don't care who I hurt or offend as long as my feelings and opinions are expressed, which is quite the opposite of Christ, who didn't ever back down from the truth, but always considered the needs of His audience. He expressed the love of God that lived inside Him, and His consideration for Himself always took a back seat to what God wanted and others needed.

Within my Christianity I have begun to realize that God is able to meet my need for self expression, and also replace that need with a desire to express Christ who is living within me. As I have discussed before in my section on relationship and communication, God is able to absorb my need for self expression, and when I pour my heart out to Him He replaces the human elements that exist there with divine comfort, peace, and joy. God knows how I feel and is receptive to hearing from me. He is also the perfect sounding board, and His spirit helps me discern the right and wrong, selfish, and valid thoughts and feelings that I have, teaching me which ones to anchor to and which ones to let go. After God helps me take care of the human need for self expression, He then reveals to me the parts of Himself that are important and dear to me. He teaches me about Himself and His ways, and His spirit produces fruit within me. I am then able to see how much more significant these qualities are than those that I develop on my own. My desire to express myself begins to seem so foolish and my desire to express Christ becomes prominent and eventually dominant in my life. When this occurs, I lose focus on myself and Christ begins to overflow and spill out of me. I can often judge the state of my relationship with Christ by how much I am interested in expressing myself, or by how much I can see Christ being expressed through me. The problem with me prioritizing expressions of myself is that I am innately self-centered, and most of the world will eventually be repulsed by me continually expressing my own desires. I am also limited by my flesh and what is important for others to receive from me, is not what I have to offer, but what Christ has to offer them through me. This is made most clear to me by experiences that I have had teaching at church. The times that I can see and feel God working through me the most, are often times when He has led me to teach on something entirely different than what I had spent the previous week preparing. During these lessons I am often amazed and humbled by what comes out of my mouth, and I am reminded that the source of the word is greater than the presenter. The simple fact is my desires must die in order for Christ's to live and be expressed through me.

One of the greatest biblical examples of this is portrayed in the life of John the Baptist. Consider the uniqueness of his situation. He was the first prophet Israel had seen in four hundred years. His personality and his ministry were so dynamic that he was able to draw large crowds away from the population centers and into the rural Jordan region where he preached. The gospels report that the people, "Went out to him;" he did not have to pursue an audience because his ministry was so popular. His message brought great repentance throughout Judea as he prepared the people's hearts for Christ. He upset the political climate of the region and eventually lost his life because the king's own household was impacted by what he had to say. He was the most charismatic and dynamic figure of his generation until Christ appeared.

As soon as John identified and baptized Christ and Jesus began his public ministry, John's following began to diminish. This was upsetting to John's disciples who pointed this fact out to him in hopes that he would do something to maintain his prominence. Instead he made one of the most humble and insightful statements in the Bible. In John chapter three, he told his disciples that he was earthly in nature and could only perform the ministry allotted to him. He stated that Christ was from Heaven and had a greater ministry that would consummate the one he had begun. His attitude at seeing Christ's ministry thrive was one of completed joy. He was able to relinquish his fame, honor, and following because he had never been intent on expressing himself, but only what God had placed inside of him. His statement to his disciples is one that should continually be lived out in our lives. He reported to them that, "He must become greater; and I must become less" (John 3:30). He had no fear at all of losing his identity to Christ. He recognized that his purpose on earth was to prepare the way for Him and that his proclamation of Christ was infinitely more important than anything he could express on his own.

The same is true of us. Expressing Christ in our lives should be a daily event. It should be natural and fulfilling.

The Road to Relationship

It should replace our need for self expression, which God in turn graciously absorbs. We don't lose our identity or uniqueness through this process. Remember it was God who created us unique, and like Jeremiah and John the Baptist, our individuality and personal features are enhanced by our expressions of Christ. We are able to express Christ in ways that are totally unique to our lives, spirits, personalities, and circumstances. God created us with very specific purposes in mind. It is also the only way that our joy can be made complete, as John's was, for pursuit of self expression is fueled by our own selfish desires and ultimately leads to strife and conflict. The simple fact is, Christ has so much more that is fruitful and positive to express in my life than I have on my own. Expressing Him brings fulfillment and renewal, while expressing myself only leaves me empty and alienated, and is ultimately a relationship killer.

We express Christ in a variety of ways. We express Him through our gifts and talents, our speech, our actions, our attitudes. The most important step in expressing Christ in our lives begins by approaching Him humbly and asking Him to work through us. When we see an opportunity to minister our first step should be prayers of submission and requests for guidance in our speech and action. Many years ago God laid a prayer on my heart that I use to this day before every lesson I teach. It goes something like this, "Father, use my efforts for your glory, and the edification of the hearers. Help them not to see, or focus on me, but to hear the words you desire to speak through me. Speak through me, Father, and help me to stay out of your way." By praying this it helps remind me that what I am about to do is for God and others, and has very little to do with me. God is faithful and each time I teach I am amazed and humbled by His desire and ability to use me.

Within our relationship God is able to absorb my need for self expression and transform it into a desire to express Christ who lives within me. This keeps our relationship in its appropriate perspective because it keeps me from becoming self-centered, which is the destructive perspective that is able to ruin my relationship with God.

WHERE WILL I SEEK GOD?

Ideally after we accept Christ, we would immediately have the understanding that He desires first and foremost an intimate relationship from us. Obviously I don't feel this is the case for most Christians, and thus the theme of this book has been my own struggle in placing relationship at the center of my Christianity. As we mature as Christians we inevitably place more and more emphasis on our relationship with Christ. This in turn provides the context for continued spiritual growth. Our spiritual growth has some of the same characteristics as our physical growth, but also some distinct differences. Unlike our physical bodies, the spiritual side of our being has no limitations or time table for maturing. How we grow in our relationship with God is quite dependent upon where and how we seek Him. God is a faithful Father and He patiently waits with all the spiritual nutrients that we need to grow up in Him. However, He does not force feed us. He is ever-present in our lives, but the level at which He allows our relationship to grow is closely related to the level of intimacy that we seek with Him. Throughout this chapter I will be referring to Exodus chapter 33, verses seven through eleven. Throughout this chapter I will also be stressing the principal that spiritual growth and intimacy with God are inseparable, and somewhat synonymous. Exodus 33:7–11 states:

> Now Moses used to take a tent and pitch it outside the camp some distance away, calling it the "tent of meeting." Anyone inquiring of the LORD would go to the tent of meeting outside the camp. And whenever Moses went out to the tent, all the people rose and stood at the entrances to their tents, watching Moses until he entered the tent. As Moses went into the tent, the pillar of cloud would come down and stay at the entrance, while the LORD spoke with Moses. Whenever the people saw the pillar of cloud standing at the entrance to the tent they all stood and worshiped each at the entrance to his tent. The LORD would speak to Moses face to face, as a man speaks with his friend. Then Moses would return to the camp, but his young aide Joshua son of Nun did not leave the tent.

Spiritual growth as a Christian is quite complex and individualized. God is working on each of our hearts at the level of intensity He knows we are ready for. He knows exactly what we are able to bear, and He will never take us beyond this point. However, often times what we feel we can bear is much less intense than what God knows we can handle. Therefore, at times, God puts us in situations that seem beyond our limits. He pulls on us and stretches us. He brings us to what we think is the limit of our faith, and shows us that through Him, we can bear more. This is not always pleasant to our flesh, but it brings life to our spirit which is fueled by the indwelling of His spirit. He is able to smash the ceiling that we have put on our faith and help us to establish a new and greater limit, which He immediately begins to target, drawing us closer to it so that He might also destroy it and reveal to us even greater victory in, and knowledge of, Him.

One distinct way that spiritual maturity can be defined is by the struggle in our life between our flesh and the Spirit. As our flesh dies, the Spirit begins to take more control of our lives. For some this can happen rather rapidly, for many it is a slow process. In I Corinthians 3:1–3, Paul refers to the members of their church as *worldly*, stating he is unable to address them as spiritual. These are people who were saved, and even had been blessed with and were using the gifts of the Spirit, but they were still more in tune with their flesh than with the Holy Spirit. This fact seems to indicate something rather obvious, that our spiritual growth is somewhat dependent upon us and the choices we make. All spiritual growth is directly attributable to God and the work He does in our lives, but the work He does is often in direct proportion to the intensity level at which we seek Him.

As I stated earlier, my deepest desire is for God to get the optimum out of my life. I don't always pursue this desire, but when my relationship with Him is being fueled, it is a driving force in my life. In Exodus chapter thirty-three, we see God's people displaying their faith in three different ways, or levels of intensity. When God's presence would come into the camp and rest in the Tent of Meeting the people had three distinct responses. Moses, the lawgiver and mediator between God and the people, would go the tent and the Lord would talk to him. When he would pass through the camp all the people would rise and go to their tents and watch as he approached the place where God came to meet with him. His relationship with God is one of nearly unparalleled intimacy in the Old Testament. He is a little picture of the Christ who was to come, listening intently to God's voice and relaying His word to the people, and pleading to the Lord to be merciful and patient with them as they lived in doubt and fear. Moses was also the ideal leader, zealous for God's reputation, boldly standing before the people and holding them accountable to God's law. Much could be written on the life of Moses, but the point that I am attempting to make is that Moses talked with God, and God talked back. He pursued God, and when He entered the tent, God's presence descended to meet him there. Moses enjoyed an incredibly close relationship with God, but the fact is that God also enjoyed and received much from this relationship. Moses received partly because he pursued, and God in His faithfulness always blesses our effort exponentially. Moses was faithful in all God's house, and because of this he experienced an intimacy beyond what any of the other Israelites even dared to imagine could be possible for themselves.

As Moses passed through the camp and all the people rose to watch him go to the tent of meeting, they would stand at the entrance of their tents and watch God's presence descend upon the tent and meet with Moses. They worshipped from the entrance to their tents. They had relationships with God, but their relationships were from a distance, it brought a blessing to them just seeing God come down to the tent of meeting, but they did not get to hear His voice, or see Him pass by, or receive His law, or fellowship with Him intimately. They were content to worship in their own tents rather than worship in the tent where God actually visited. They were content to get God's words from Moses instead of receiving them from the Lord's own lips. They treated God much like we do in twenty-first century America, they acknowledged His power and His sovereignty, they had seen Him work and they were His people, but they continued to be stiff-necked and stubborn, trying to hang on to their flesh and never fully letting go of their homes in Egypt, the land of their slavery. Like us, they began their journey with God much more in tune with their human nature than they were with the spiritual reality that exists beyond our flesh. They were content with this dynamic however, and they continued to see the world with their finite human eyes instead of the spiritual eyes that God gave Moses, and that He desperately wanted to give to them. They never ceased to be the people of God and they bore His name to their graves, but they died in a desert when God had prepared them a land flowing with milk and honey. They missed their destiny because their relationship lacked the personal connection that God desires. They were content from a distance, despite the fact that verse seven of Exodus thirty-three tells us that anyone could go to the Tent of Meeting and inquire of the Lord. Their lack of intimacy with God, despite all his work, characterized their generation and made them a tragic example of what God does not want from His people.

The third character described in this chapter is Joshua, who at the time was serving as Moses' aide. In this chapter, we do not see Joshua experiencing the same type of relationship that Moses had with God. He was not spoken to personally, he was not given the law, and he was not allowed to watch God pass by. However, he was not content to worship God from the entrance of his tent back in the camp. Verse eleven tells us that after God spoke to Moses that he would return to the people in the camp, but that Joshua who had accompanied him to the Tent of Meeting, "Did not leave the tent." Joshua may not have had the intimate relationship that Moses had with God, but he was unwilling to stay in his own tent and worship God from afar. He followed Moses and he went into the Tent of Meeting. Regardless of the fact that God did not speak to him directly, Joshua sought to be in His presence and even when Moses left the tent, Joshua stayed behind, because that was the place that God came down to meet with man. He pursued God, and was willing to take from Him anything that he could get—even if it was the scraps from the relationship that Moses had with God. His efforts were not unrewarded, and he found out that when it comes to a relationship with God; He doesn't give scraps, but instead pours out blessings that are individualized to our unique hearts, fulfilling our dearest needs and our most desperate desires. Joshua's relationship with God was not what Moses' relationship was at that time because Moses had a longer history with God. Joshua's pursuit of God and his desire to stay where God's presence dwelt paid off in many wonderful ways in his life. He became the man that led God's people into the land of promise, God did eventually speak to him directly, and he experienced the intimate presence of God that he so dearly pursued alone in the Tent of Meeting.

The Road to Relationship

These three types of responses to God that we see in Exodus are not unlike the responses that we have in our present day and age. I am constantly presented with the same question that the Israelites were, "Where will I seek God?" I want desperately for my life to reflect the answer that my heart instinctively gives, which is, "In the place that His presence dwells." My human nature pulls at me from the entrance to my fleshly tent and attempts to make me comfortable where I am at, and even reminds me of the fact that the pleasures of my flesh exist back in Egypt, or in my case, back in the main stream of our worldly culture. I'm more fortunate than the generation of Israelites that died in the desert, because I have God living inside of me in the form of His spirit. His presence is always available to me and, like Moses, I can have a most wonderfully intimate fellowship with Him. When I do experience this I am reminded that there is nothing at all the world has to offer that is so precious and satisfying. I am strengthened and energized, and am able to go and minister just as Moses was able to—in God's strength and with the confidence that only an intimate relationship with Him can provide. At times my flesh continues to battle me fiercely, and I may not necessarily feel God's presence or see His blessings, but like Joshua I must be unwilling to leave the place that He dwells pursuing what I know only He can give, and even though I may not see or realize it now, I can take comfort in the fact that my pursuit of God will not go unrewarded. Like Joshua, God's greatest blessings and my greatest work may be ahead of me, but they both begin with me being unwilling to leave the tent where God's presence dwells.

CONCLUSION

Relationship, it is so simple and intimate and the thing that we were created for, yet so foreign to our flesh and often elusive to our forms of Christianity. My road to relationship has been rocky at times, painful to my flesh, and often detoured by my own wants and desires. Despite this, I am desperately thankful for every step along that road that God has allowed me to take because each one ultimately brings me close to the intimacy I long for with Him, and that He desires with me. Relationship is the center of our Christianity, if anything else is at the center then God is being cheated out of the exact thing that He sent His son to achieve. God is able to provide us with a closeness that exceeds anything a friend, a child, or even a spouse can produce in our lives. He enjoys our fellowship, and through Christ He is able to see us as sinless friends that He wants to talk to and also hear from. He is a perfect friend, and each second that we spend with Him returns on us blessings beyond measure, unable to be produced by any human. A relationship with Him provides joy, peace, contentment, satisfaction, and an ever-growing knowledge of the Holy God of the Universe who sits upon His thrown and rules over all creation, and yet takes personal interest in all that I say, do, feel, and think.

God's desire and the work of Christ as our perfect sacrifice have provided us with a gift and opportunity that is truly indescribable. We have the presence of God living inside of us, and we have a relationship with Him that is unhindered by our sin. If Abraham, Moses, David, Jeremiah, or any of the Old Testament figures could have seen into the future and grasped the position we have in Christ and the blessing of the indwelling of the Spirit, they would have traded places with us in a heart beat. Only our flesh hinders our relationship with God. Any uncleanness that we experience from our sin is forgiven upon confession, and God's grace is massively abundant and lavishly poured out upon us, to have *life to the full* we need only accept the spiritual realities that God has provided and walk in them daily.

I have come to one of the most exciting conclusions of my life. *Religion is not the most important aspect of my life, relationship is.* There is great freedom in Christ that I have foolishly resisted and even fought against in the past. I am freed from ceremony and ritual, I have no way to make myself right with God because my God is too great for a mere man to be able to achieve such a thing in a relationship with Him. I don't have to focus on sinning less, or working harder, or worshipping more intensely, or becoming consumed by my circumstances—all I have to do is pursue intimate fellowship with my loving Creator, Savior, and Father. He is near and He desires my attention and my companionship more than anything else I can give Him. At times I have to get alone with Him, leave my Bible on the shelf, put up my prayer list, stop singing songs, and just *be still and know that He is God*, meditate on Him, and allow Him to begin the divine communication that my soul hungers for, that I can get from no other source or means. I must spend intimate time with God, for He desires the fellowship that only I can give Him, for there is only one me, created in His heart and mind and chosen before the creation of the world to be saved by the blood of His precious only son. It's still hard to accept, but God has an incredible yearning from deep within His heart to have a relationship with me. Nothing in all the world is more dear to my heart or exciting to my spirit than this fact, and my greatest desire and new prayer is that He will receive from my life and our relationship exactly what He wants, and that He will be able to enjoy me as a Father enjoys his son, and a man his close friend.

I still get confused, frustrated, and angry. My flesh still dogs me, tirelessly waiting for me to give it an opening. I stumble and fall, I lose my way, I allow my emotions to lie to me and sometimes I end up making decisions based on what I feel instead of what I know to be true. Despite these facts, there is absolutely nothing that is so pleasing to me as to drink of the endless cup of God's fellowship. Like Jacob I have pursued a life that I want. Even though I may have been conscious of God and even pursued His blessings, I have at times lived a life of putrid compromise being pulled by my flesh and His spirit. However, just like Jacob, when I was mercifully taken to the point where I had nothing else to depend on, I grabbed a hold of God and I will not let go of Him ever again. The struggle persists, but my flesh is losing ground and the wrestling match that we have been in has mostly been replaced by loving embraces. I may not be all that I or God desire me to be, but like Joshua I am unwilling to leave the place where God dwells, and my hope is that someday my relationship with Him will bring Him the great joy and satisfaction that He so desires.